ONLY THE STRONG THRIVE

A True Story of Struggle, Perseverance, and Triumph

APRIL H. COLLINS

Only the Strong Thrive:
A True Story of Struggle, Perseverance, and Triumph
Copyright © by April H. Collins

Requests for information should be emailed to:

author@onlythestrongthrive.com

All Scripture quotations, unless otherwise indicated, are taken from the ESV® Bible (the Holy Bible, English Standard Version®, copyright © 2001 by Crossway, a publishing ministry of Good News Publishers. Used by permission. All rights reserved. Scripture taken from the New King James Version®. Copyright © 1982 by Thomas Nelson. Used by permission. All rights reserved. Scriptures taken from the Holy Bible, New International Version®, NIV®, Copyright © 1973, 1978, 1984, 2011 by Biblica, Inc.™ Used by permission of Zondervan. All rights reserved.

Hardback ISBN: 978-1-7325473-1-5
Paperback ISBN: 978-1-7325473-0-8
eBook ISBN: 978-1-7325473-2-2

All rights reserved. No part of this book may be reproduced or transmitted in any form or by any means, electronic or mechanical, including photocopying and recording, or by any information storage or retrieval system, without permission in writing from the publisher.

Published in the United States by April H. Collins

Printed in the United States

onlythestrongthrive.com
facebook.com/authoraprilhcollins
twitter.com/author_acollins

For My Children,
Jaylen, Ava, Aryn & Warren.

"Don't set boundaries on your heart when your options are limitless."

Because of my Husband,
Quincy,

and my Sister-in-Christ,
Felicia.

*You are the reason words are on these pages.
I'm forever grateful.
"God's mission is accomplished through everyday relationships."*

Contents

Introduction

1 To Survive or to Thrive? That is the Question.

2 Strength in Adversity: A Glance at My Story

3 The Strength to Conquer Fear

4 Strong Faith

5 The Strength to Focus

6 The Strength to Forgive and Be Free

7 The Strength to Love

8 Strength in Community

9 The Strength to Move Forward

10 The Strength to Triumph

INTRODUCTION

"Only the strong survive."

I think it's safe to say that at one point or another—as an adult or perhaps even as a child—many of us have heard this saying. Four words so popular that 1960s soul crooner Jerry Butler put music with them and made a hit song.

Sometimes we might utter those words after overcoming obstacles, conquering challenges, and beating odds. We have the tendency to victoriously say, "Only the strong survive!" to affirm that it took strength to get through a difficult time; strength that we might not have realized we possessed.

As young children, many of us have elaborate plans and dreams for our futures. At that tender age, we rarely think about the challenges that might lay ahead. Our circumstances, regardless

Introduction

how bleak, rarely stop us from dreaming as children. At some point though, we begin to understand life's challenges, and we might even become intimidated by them. Over time, our dreams might move to the backs of our minds; and sometimes, the challenges make us forget about our goals and dreams altogether. However, if we postpone our dreams, the strength we need to pursue them might be consumed just trying to survive.

In the midst of life's challenges, we may not always feel strong, but we know we certainly need strength to survive. Most of us don't want to just *survive* though, we want to *succeed!* It takes true strength to succeed at life. Only the strong *thrive!*

When I think about the word "thrive," I can't help but reflect on that great day when I sat nervously, yet extremely proud, waiting to hear my name announced. Finally, after what seemed like forever, I heard "April V. Houston," from the microphone. For a second or two I was paralyzed by the joy and excitement of the moment, but when I gathered myself, I sauntered across the stage to accept my law degree. As I strolled across the stage to rousing cheers from

Only the Strong Thrive

family and friends, thoughts of the preceding twenty years overwhelmed me. That short walk meant more than just earning my law degree. It was a moment that seemed to bring purpose to the past twenty years.

I wondered, "How could this poor little girl from a small city be standing here today?" This was the same little girl who suffered years of childhood trauma. This was the little girl who was raised by a single father; a girl who had to rely on government assistance for most of her life—even through law school; a girl who had a child of her own before she was old enough to provide for herself. Yet, this girl was finally right there, dancing in her own dream.

I decided to write this book to share my life's experiences and the challenges I overcame to finally learn to live a fulfilled life. I want to give hope to those who wish to do more than just survive. I want to give hope to those, who despite their circumstance, have a desire to *thrive*.

I believe we are all empowered to live abundant and purposeful lives. Through this

Introduction

book, I illustrate how we can each find the strength to push through adversity and live out our dreams. I understand some of us may have been dealt an unfortunate hand. Some of us were born into terrible circumstances, while others have lived through devastating situations that have occurred at other points in life. Despite life's circumstances, we each have the power to activate a source of strength that can all but erase the years of disappointment and distress.

The good news is we've already been given the key to happiness, peace, joy, and the freedom we desire for our lives. We need only to unlock the door. Jesus Christ is our door. We can thrive and live our best lives because of the perfect life He lived. In His love for us, we have all we need. Yet, there are still actions we must take – some things we can do – to give ourselves the best chance to live out our hopes and dreams.

Each chapter in this book purposely begins with a Bible verse to focus your heart and mind before you explore the contents. These are scriptures that have consistently comforted, encouraged, and inspired me when I've gone through trials. I pray they will encourage you the same way they have encouraged me. Hopefully, you will revisit them for strength when you feel weak.

My use of the word "strength" throughout this book is not limited to our physical strength. It is the strength of God's power that can work in each of us. It is His strength that has gotten me through challenging situations. My experiences have taught me—and hopefully they will serve the same purpose for you—that I can trust God in my weakness to make me strong.

"His power is made perfect in our weakness" (2 Corinthians 12:9).

My unwavering trust in God did not come easily. There were times when trusting God was not my first choice. It's easy to rely on our own strength to remedy a challenging situation, but I've realized when we allow God's strength to work in us, in all areas of our lives, we will thrive! His strength becomes our strength and with it we can overcome adversity.

Introduction

I'm certain most of us have been hurt or have experienced something we believed would kill us. If you have not, continue living; that time will come. Sometimes we are the authors of our fate; in other cases, we are the victims of the choices other people make. How we choose to live, despite those actions, is significant. We must call on our faith to give us the strength to forgive and to heal from the wounds of abuse, rejection, and mistreatment. When we choose to forgive, we free ourselves from the mental and emotional chains that keep us from moving forward. I realize it is easier said than done, but God's strength gives us what we need to keep moving.

Finally, we cannot discount the collective strength of family and our individual community to help us live fulfilled lives. Our journeys are not designed to be traveled alone. Contrary to the way many of us were raised as children, it is okay to ask for and to accept help. In fact, we need help to move closer to our destinies. Our greatest leaders were not successful alone. I so often think of the Civil Rights leaders who worked together to accomplish their goals. They were stronger together. Even Jesus had a community with His disciples working alongside Him here on earth.

With these things in mind, I hope you are inspired to use your strength in God to successfully conquer whatever obstacles are in your way.

"We are more than conquerors through Him who loved us" (Romans 8:37).

It's your time to thrive!

1

TO THRIVE OR TO SURVIVE?

THAT IS THE QUESTION.

"I am come that they might have life, and that they might have it more abundantly."

John 10:10

The phrase "Only the strong survive" is often used to describe an individual's physical or mental ability to overcome a challenge. It originates from the scientific concept "survival of the fittest," which was a concept used by 19th century biologist Charles Darwin to define his theory of natural selection. According to the theory, those who best adapt to their immediate environment will survive. The determining factor in one's ability to survive depends on heritable traits.

Our lives are more than a scientific concept. Physical traits do not determine our ability to succeed. They have bearing on some things in our lives, but our traits do not determine whether we can live abundant lives. Effort and energy are required to thrive.

Our ability to thrive depends on what we do with what we have been given. It's our choice whether to thrive or to survive. Thank God science is not the end all be all. It doesn't matter if we were born into the most unfortunate circumstances, we can choose to live abundant lives filled with love, joy, peace, and happiness. However, it doesn't happen haphazardly. We must work for it.

To Thrive or to Survive?

To live abundantly we should first discover our life's purpose. Discovering our purpose may be difficult sometimes. We can become so consumed with surviving that we fail to understand or realize our life's purpose. Our day-to-day tasks can become overwhelming and exhaust our energy to dream and move toward our goals. Though these tasks are necessary, they don't always push us to living life abundantly. We must make purposeful and defined steps that will ultimately help us reach our desired life goals.

Those steps rarely lead to swift or immediate success, but if we keep moving forward we can overcome the obstacles that many times end in disappointment, heartaches, or failures. We *can* break the cycle. We must no longer be content with living a life of survival.

I know what it feels like to just survive. The first twenty years of my life were filled with chaos, hurt, heartache, abuse, and confusion. Those were the days I survived. I survived, witnessing more domestic violence episodes than I could count. I survived, when my dad, a single father, was away serving jail time on drug charges. I survived, when my brothers and I only had the Ramen noodles my granddad dropped off to ensure we had food to eat. I survived, when the instability of moving from place to place was all too common. I survived, when I was tasked with entering a phase of motherhood, caring for my infant brother, at twelve years old. I survived years of sexual abuse at the hands of someone I should've been able to trust. Again, I understand what it means to survive.

Surviving is not easy. The energy we put into it will expend us and leave us with nothing. Thankfully, there is more to life than surviving. This was not the life I wanted to continue to live. I was determined to thrive.

The Best Life

After giving birth to my son at 18 years old, it became clear that I had to do something with my life. It wasn't just about me anymore. I needed to make the best life for my child.

To Thrive or to Survive?

Making the best life for him was not limited to ensuring his physical needs were met. I knew there was more to his life than providing the best clothes or buying him the most expensive pair of tennis shoes. It was not about making sure he had access to the material things I didn't have while growing up. Making the best life for him meant pursuing my educational goals and building a solid spiritual foundation. Those were the necessary steps I took to put him on a path of opportunity and promise. Making the best life for him meant reaching the highest levels I could reach in all aspects of my life.

Reaching the highest levels in anything requires us to engage the strength we all possess, take the initial steps, and work diligently. We must focus our minds on the goal and be determined that nothing will stop us.

Our vision can become distorted and cause us to lose sight of the dreams that were once so important. Obstacles may come our way and take us off course, but we must not lose sight of our goals.

Only the Strong Thrive

It's typical to question ourselves and our ability to navigate through challenges. We may question our strength and automatically think the challenge is greater. Too often, when we're trying to determine whether we can reach the goals we've always dreamed of, we use outdated and inaccurate information. We look at our past, who we used to be, and the things we used to do. It discourages us.

We will even allow the words of others to define our ability to reach our goals. You may be able to recall the discouraging words you've heard, *"Oh, you used to do..."*, or *"You won't be able to do that because..."* Words are powerful, and those words somehow become engraved in our minds.

We may also let statistics impact our desire in reaching our goals and aspirations. If numbers and formulas had it their way, they would have told many of us *"No!" "It's not going to happen,"* and *" You can't."* However, we cannot let statistics nullify our dreams.

To Thrive or to Survive?

Statistics don't always work in our favor, especially for those who, like me, have been marginalized because of our socioeconomic backgrounds. Statistics would have many of us to believe we are less likely to go to college, less likely to marry, and less likely to have financial stability.

For a long time, my life contributed to the statistics we never want to define us. However, I refused to be the person defined by statistics and defined by others. I made the decision to define my life. Thankfully, my dreams were bigger than what others saw for my future.

Little Girl Big Dreams

When I was a little girl, roaming the halls of elementary and middle school in my small hometown, I dreamed of my future. I had the same dream as many of my peers at the time. I wanted to be wealthy, drive a luxury car, and live in a big house.

Those dreams helped me deal with my

Only the Strong Thrive

troubled reality. My mind would take me to better places. I didn't have much of an imagination, but I had enough to dream. I wanted to be an attorney, be married at 23, be the mother of twin girls at 26, have cooks and maids, and live in a mansion next door to my cousin. I had everything laid out so perfectly.

But as I grew older, I discovered it wasn't that simple. There was much more to living an abundant life than what I drove, how much money I made, and where I lived. I realized fulfillment in life was not in the tangible or material accomplishments. Fulfillment came by watching God work miracles in the midst of darkness. It came in knowing I could trust Him to give me the desires of my heart. However, I learned quickly God was not just going to give me what I wished. I had work to do as well. I had to prepare myself for a long journey.

Before I could work to get the desires of my heart, I needed to know what those desires were. My dreams and goals needed to be evident. We must always know where we are going before we begin our journey. It's the same as taking a road

To Thrive or to Survive?

trip.

My husband and I try to take our children on as many road trips as we possibly can. As part of our initial planning, we've always identified our destination first. I've never been the type of person who could get in the car and start driving with no destination in mind, especially not with children. There are those who can, but it would not be ideal for me.

Before we pack our bags, and before we put all the children in the car, we routinely use Google Maps to determine the direction we will be traveling and how long it will take to make it to our destination. We do this for several reasons. First, we need to have a general idea of the route and the roads we'll be traveling. We also need to know where to find a good resting point along the journey. We have to factor in restroom visits and food breaks because with our four children, we know we will have to stop often.

Even though Google Maps provides the route and estimated travel time, we must consider much more based on our personal situation. However, knowing our desired destination is the first part of our planning process. It is the same in life; we must plan, organize and execute.

Prior planning won't completely shield us from mishaps. No matter how perfectly we plan each trip, sometimes our plans are thwarted. Inevitably, there will be a roadblock, a stalled vehicle, a car accident, or something blocking the roadway. Three-hour trips have easily turned into five. Ten-hour trips have turned into twelve hours. But that didn't stop us from arriving at our destination. We were oftentimes rerouted on the map to take a different direction. Moving from six-lane highways to two-lane roads have slowed us down, but we always made it to our destination... with a story to tell.

Each time we've reached our destinations, thoughts of the long journey move to the backs of our minds as excitement, joy, and smiles fill our faces. Like road trips, our life stories are made along the journey.

To Thrive or to Survive?

Roadblocks and challenges are frustrating as we pursue our big dreams. The time and effort that we expend can be overwhelming as well. However, the rewards will always exceed the difficulties we encounter along the way.

2

STRENGTH IN ADVERSITY:

A GLANCE AT MY STORY

"We are afflicted in every way, but not crushed; perplexed, but not driven to despair; persecuted, but not forsaken; struck down, but not destroyed."

2 Corinthians 4:8-9

I'm an 80s baby and not just any 80s baby. I'm one that will proudly wear a t-shirt to

Strength in Adversity

exclaim it. That scenario may be completely different in a few more years. I may not want to so boldly and proudly display my age for all to see. Whether I choose to share my age or reserve it for must-have occasions doesn't really matter. I can't change the fact I was born in the 1980s. Therefore, it would be pointless to complain about my birth date or use it as an excuse or hindrance. Instead of being disgruntled, it is better to try to understand how being born in that decade has impacted my life and how it has shaped my view of the world.

The mindset we must have about when we were born, must be the same mindset we have about the circumstances into which we were born. Some of us have many reasons to be discontent about the situations surrounding our lives from the day we were born. We can either complain about it, or we can embrace it and allow ourselves to understand how those conditions helped shape us. We can choose to exert our energy in negative places of regret and resentment, or we can use those circumstances as a source of strength to make a better life.

When I reflect on my childhood, I recall a

time that was without hope from the beginning. My parents were young, poor children who ventured into a relationship and later a marriage that was not healthy. I was born out of those complexities.

They met at the nightclub my granddad owned. At the time my dad was eighteen and my mom was only thirteen. My mother was a young teen, but she was a regular guest there. By the age of fifteen, she was pregnant and gave birth to her first child. Soon after giving birth to my brother, I was born.

Having two children so close in age, while in high school, was difficult for her. As a result, she dropped out in the eleventh grade. Two years later, my younger brother was born. My parents were young and in love, but at their age, I don't think they fully understood true love or the responsibilities of providing a stable home for their children.

The years we lived together as a family were filled with constant uncertainty and distress.

Strength in Adversity

Unfortunately, my parents fought constantly—and their disagreements were not limited to verbal disagreements. Their disputes escalated frequently. Several times they ended with my mother fleeing the state with my brothers and me, whether by bus or by hitching a ride in the cab of an 18-wheeler.

I often witnessed irons, pots, and pans thrown around. Physical altercations became my new normal and they didn't only occur behind the closed doors of our home. I can recall several fights that occurred while one or the other were driving—with my brothers and I riding as passengers. I was mortified when one my elementary school teachers happened to pull over to stop a road-side fight between the two of them. For years, I shamefully lowered my head every time I saw her. I often wondered if she thought less of me because of the way my parents behaved.

My parents' fights did not end at fists and words. The use of knives and guns eventually became my reality too. Witnessing my mother shoot at my father is an event that will forever be etched in my mind. Seeing the red and bloodied gash on his leg from an incident of her severely stabbing him are childhood memories I will never forget.

Despite the levels of violence and trauma my brothers and I endured, we never called the police. 911 was the very last number we would have ever dialed, even in our most vulnerable moments during their fights. There was an unspoken rule about calling the police. We would have let my parents kill each other before we made that call. The only person my brothers and I felt comfortable calling to calm the situation was my granddad. His number was the first one we would dial. He always came to the rescue.

I'll never forget the fights; the fear in my heart that one of them would kill the other. Memories of the small three-bedroom house we lived in during my early elementary school days won't ever be forgotten.

However, it wasn't all bad. There weren't fights every day. We had good times there too. I remember our first Christmas there. The decorated Christmas tree, with presents underneath, made me feel like a "normal" kid. I remember playing in the neighborhood with cousins and friends. We'd ride bikes, climb trees, sing, and make up dance routines. We'd try so hard to imitate the dance moves of performers like Another Bad Creation, Vanilla Ice, and Xscape. We'd explore the nearby wooded areas and make up stories about the "creepy" homes we saw in the distance.

I remember my beautiful bedroom too. After we moved, I never had another room like it again. My mom had so thoughtfully decorated it in my favorite color: purple. She picked out the most unique white canopy-style bed, draped it with light purple bedding and a sheer bed curtain hanging from the top. The white furniture with the purple accessories made the perfect combination. It was a room for a little princess. Sometimes I would just stare at the charming picture of the little fenced-in white house she hung beside my bed. I loved my bedroom, and it was truly my sanctuary from the troubles.

Tragically, before long, it became the venue for another unforgettable childhood memory.

Locked Away

My parents separated when I was about nine years old. My dad suddenly and unexpectantly became an unemployed, single father of three children. Knowing he had three little mouths to feed, he resorted to extreme measures to take care of us. It wasn't unusual for him to be away from home for most of the day and night, leaving my brothers and I home alone. There were times my brothers and I would have to 'shoo' away strangers at our door step in the late-night hours. We learned to protect our home and one another at an early age.

One night, we heard a car driving up the gravel road that led to our duplex. Thinking it was our dad returning home, we peeked out of the window. Just one peek and we immediately stopped breathing and dropped to the floor. In a panic, we crawled to the back room. It wasn't our dad. It was the police! As one officer knocked on the door, the other crept around the duplex shining a flashlight into all the windows. We listened intently to their whispers but couldn't understand what they were saying. Although they were probably only there for a matter of minutes, with our breathless and motionless bodies crouched against the base of the bedroom wall, it felt like they scoped out the duplex for hours.

As soon as we heard them shut the patrol car door and travel back down the gravel driveway, we all burst into loud cries of terror. Our little pounding hearts did not know what to think. We'd never experienced any positive interactions with the police. We knew their presence meant something bad.

Who are they looking for?

Is our dad okay?

Something had to be wrong. I dialed my granddad's phone number faster than my brain could think. He was there within a matter of minutes. After reaching my dad on his car phone, our hearts were put at ease.

Though the incident that night ended well, my dad was arrested on drug charges a couple of times and served time in jail during my elementary and middle school years. Learning he had been included in a drug "bust" brought a dark cloud over me. Even at that age, it was humbling to know he'd been picked up in a police van and likely paraded around the neighborhood as I'd too often seen happen to others.

The shame was stinging. In my eyes, he stood on a pedestal—above all others. He was our hero, our provider, our protector. I never had to worry about ill-treatment from anyone in the "streets" because they knew my dad. He was my shield of defense, and now he was gone—locked away. I not only had to process it internally, but I had to deal with outside factors as well.

I hated riding the school bus after my dad's incarceration because my brother and I would have to endure jokes about it. The long, miserable bus-rides were bound to start and end with chuckles, questions and statements like, "*Where's your dad?*" "*He ain't getting out!*"

The tears were inside, but I would have never let anyone see my broken heart. Even though my brother was older, I felt like I had to put on a strong front for him. I learned to disguise my feelings very well.

My dad's time away left a void. His lack of physical presence meant an absence of structure, which ultimately became a "free for all" for me. I was back and forth between family members' homes, and there weren't many consistent eyes on me to make sure I was on the right path. As a result, I started hanging with an older crowd.

More Trouble

I learned a lot during the summer before my sixth-grade year. It was an adventurous time, to say the least. I woke up every morning with no one telling me what I had to do for the day. Whatever was on my older friends' agenda for the day was on mine. Many days consisted of riding on the backs of trucks, exploring the city while smoking marijuana. My friends tried to teach me how to inhale and exhale, but I could never really get the hang of it. Out of all the days

Only the Strong Thrive

I tried to get "high," I only remember feeling different once. I knew the effect it had on my friends though. We would always stop at Food World for snacks and fill the aisles with lots of laughter and entertainment.

After my parents' separation, my brothers and I rarely spent time with my mother. However, when my dad was incarcerated, we moved in with her for a short time. A few days after my father was rounded up in the police van, my mother revealed to us that she was pregnant. "*Pregnant?*" I thought. I didn't know how to feel about it. I barely had time to even process my father's incarceration. I experienced a mixture of emotions. For one, I was certain the baby-to-be was not my father's child. Despite the problems that led to their separation, hearing she was having a baby with another man was a lot for my young mind to process. I couldn't wrap my head around it all.

We were already in a terrible situation with my father being in jail. A new baby in an already fractured family would make life even more difficult for all of us. I had no idea what would follow. After my youngest brother was born, I immediately became like a mother to him. The responsibility fell on me because my mother had to work. I didn't have a clue about mixing formula or changing diapers, but I quickly got the hang of it.

When my father was finally released from jail he came to get us. I initially thought the responsibility of rearing my youngest sibling would no longer be mine. The same day my dad came home from jail, he moved us into one room at my granddad's house. The four of us slept together in my deceased grandmother's king bed.

Shortly after getting as settled as we could get, my mother arrived at my granddad's home in a U-Haul truck to drop my baby brother off. I didn't realize she had dropped him off to live with us permanently, but I quickly learned that to be the case. He really became like my child from then on. I gave up extracurricular activities because I didn't have the time or the energy to participate in them. Getting home from school to cook, clean, wash clothes, feed and take care of my little brother left barely enough time for homework. As a pre-teen, I learned what it meant to set priorities.

Small Steps

I didn't only feel the brunt of my mother's absence because of the loads of extra physical responsibility I took on when she left, but I also felt it emotionally. I felt abandoned and alone. I missed out on the mother-daughter bonding moments I saw shared between my friends and their mothers. I yearned for that relationship. I desperately needed the mother-daughter talks, especially during my teenage years. I missed the shoulder to cry on when I felt like my dad just didn't understand. Many times, I needed an advocate. I longed to have that someone who would stand up for me and be the mediator who would calm the waters between my dad and me.

Strength in Adversity

When I became a teenager, I often reflected upon my early childhood with resentment. I felt like my childhood had been squandered because of the bad choices of others. But what could I do? Initially, I maintained. I did what I was told. I went along with the demands. However, by the time I reached high school, things changed.

I became a rebel without a cause at home. At school, I was still a very good student. On the outside, I appeared to be the typical teenager, but on the inside, it was a very different story. Being the only girl in the house started to take its toll. I grew weary of being the caretaker. I just wanted to be a teenager. I wanted to be able to do teenage things without so much responsibility. I was bitter, angry, and I felt unsupported. As a result, I turned to peers for the support I felt I wasn't getting at home. Whenever I was given an inch of freedom, I took a mile. That's where my personal struggles began.

I became pregnant in the twelfth grade and delivered my son right before college was to begin. That made my life even more complicated. I could not do anything but survive. I was tired and confused. It was hard making ends meet with a newborn and a minimum wage job. Luckily, low income housing and food stamps were just enough to keep us sheltered and fed.

At the time, it felt like I was moving about aimlessly, yet by remaining enrolled in college, I was still taking one little wobbly step at a time toward my goals.

Eventually, I graduated from college and enrolled in law school. It wasn't until I stepped foot into my first law school class at the age of twenty-four that I begin to see the impact that each of those small steps had on where I was at the moment. I finally felt like I was strategically moving toward the dreams I envisioned when I was just a young girl. It was really happening, but I could not forget what led me to this point.

3

THE STRENGTH TO CONQUER FEAR

"For God hath not given us the spirit of fear; but of power, and of love, and of a sound mind."

2 Timothy 1:7

I have never been as fearful as I was when I found out I was pregnant in the twelfth grade. Despite the years of turmoil and my rebellion at home, I excelled in school and had already been accepted into college. But when the morning sickness and physical changes started, I was pretty sure college was going to take a back seat.

Pregnancy symptoms hit me like a ton of bricks one night while out celebrating New Year's Eve with friends. Although I'd never experienced pregnancy before, with the rapid onset of body aches, back pain, and nausea, I immediately thought I might be pregnant.

I was scared. I didn't know what it would mean for my future. To be honest, I was just as terrified of what my dad would do to me when he found out. The only thing I could do to buy some time was to hide my pregnancy, and I did for over four months. If I could've hidden my pregnancy the entire time, I probably would have. However, I soon learned there's only so long a body developing a baby can go without the proper rest and nutrition...and sweatshirts start to look suspicious in the spring-time.

The Strength to Conquer Fear

Keeping my pregnancy a secret was eating away at me. I tried to maintain, but it became more and more difficult by the day. Getting up in the morning for school was a task within itself. I don't know how I passed first period Calculus. I seemed to have missed more classes than I attended. Thankfully, I had co-op in the afternoon and could leave early.

Every day, I went home and "crashed" on the couch to try to energize before going to my fast food job. The morning sickness, classwork, homework, work, taking care of my little brother, and household duties all became more than I could handle. One night, while working my regular shift, I fainted and was taken to the emergency room.

In my mind I knew there wasn't going to be much more hiding my pregnancy after the ER visit. On the one hand, I didn't want to face the fear of revealing my four-month long secret. However, on the other hand, it almost came as a relief. I felt as if I now had an "excuse" to reveal it.

Only the Strong Thrive

After arriving at the hospital, the first thing the nurse asked for was a urine sample. The slow and unsteady walk to the restroom felt like an eternal hallway lined with doors of anxiety, fear, and disappointment. I didn't need the sample to tell me what I already knew but hearing it from a nurse made it more of a reality. I felt forced to address it all in those moments.

While lying on the hospital bed, I thought about one hundred different ways to break the news to my dad. None of them seemed good enough to eliminate the fear of the consequences I knew I would have to face. I'd had my fair share of physical punishment over the years, and I knew for sure I'd have to brace myself for another episode. I wondered how my body would survive it with a fetus growing inside.

Fortunately, the nurse came back into the room. As she placed a monitor on my stomach, she unknowingly rescued me from my agonizing train of thought. From the monitor I heard life from within my body for the first time. The loud 'swooshing' and fast-paced thumping sounds could not have been any more real.

It was *my* baby.

With each heartbeat, I gained more courage to say what I knew needed to be said. After making it home from the hospital, I told my aunt.

"I already knew. I was just waiting for you to say something," she replied.

I immediately thought how easy it would have been to respond to a question about my growing abdomen rather than to have to reveal it this way. But no one asked, and now was not the time to dwell on the "what-ifs". Instead, I asked her to help me reveal it to my dad, and she did. It was one of the hardest conversations I've ever had in my life.

Breaking the News

After breaking the news to my dad, he instructed me to call my mom. I rolled my eyes. She had not been present in our lives for a while, so I didn't fully understand the need to do so. Nonetheless, he made me do it.

Only the Strong Thrive

Upon hearing the news, my mother cried. She was hurt and disappointed. I could not sympathize with her or even fully understand her feelings initially. I was resentful towards her for not being in our lives, but her next statement served as the turning point in the way I felt.

"I don't want you to end up like me."

Hearing her words made me think a little more about her disappointment. She became pregnant at an early age, dropped out of high school, and never graduated. She didn't want her only daughter to experience the same disappointments she endured. I understood.

However, what she suggested next was not something I ever expected to hear.

"Have an abortion."

I could not believe my ears. Our relationship was strained, but I realized a mother would consider nearly anything to try to protect her child. Her recommendation was her attempt to guide me toward a better life—a better life than she'd had. This was her effort to keep me on the path of high school graduation and college. She saw it as a way to save my future.

Having an abortion would have given me a way out of the physical and emotional barriers I knew I would have to face. It would have eliminated my fear of being a parent. Having an abortion would have erased my fear of not being able to move forward with my life as what I would have described as "normal." I was on the cusp of celebrating a major milestone in my life, graduating from high school. Having a baby should not have been a concern of mine. My energy should have been devoted toward preparing for college.

As apprehensive as I was about my inability to pursue my goals and dreams, and as fearful as I was about how I was going to take care of a little baby, I said, *"No, I'm not having an abortion, but I'm still going to graduate from high school and go to college."* Amid my fear, I made a promise to myself, and I vowed to keep that promise.

Being fearful of how my life would change was

one thing. Fearing my parents' response to their teen daughter's pregnancy was another. Wondering how the community and church community would now look at me was a different monster. Like most teenagers, I wanted to be accepted. I feared my teenage pregnancy would cause me to be rejected, and I was terrified.

The week of spring break was the week I told my parents. It seemed like the entire world knew of my pregnancy in a matter of days. When I returned to school Monday morning, it felt like I was the talk of the school. Many of my peers approached me to share who said what about me and my pregnancy.

"They thought she was going to go do something with her life and look at her now."

"Oh, we knew she wasn't going to do anything with herself."

Hearing statements like those became all too common. I heard it all. This was the very thing I was afraid would happen. I didn't know how to handle it. It was unbearable. The unfortunate thing was knowing I was helpless. I could not do anything about anyone's opinion of me.

It would have been easy for me to give up and continue to subject myself to the negativity. Who could have blamed me for believing everything others said to be true? Instead, I made the conscious decision to use the negativity as fuel, fuel to power my dreams. I made the decision to kick fear in the face, graduate from high school, and enroll in college.

Defining Fear

Conquering fear isn't something that's mastered in high school, though. To be honest, there is no defined time when fear is ever conquered. In many instances, overcoming fear is a process. For me and my high school experience, it was just the beginning. Fear seemed to always find a way to emerge from the darkness over the years. I believe it does the same to even the most fearless person. Fear can cripple and prevent us from living abundant lives.

Only the Strong Thrive

It usually rears its ugly head when we desire to better ourselves.

I remember after years of working as a federal investigator, I envisioned establishing my own law practice. Long before thoughts of opening my own practice began, I told myself, *"I will never open my own law practice." "It's too much work,"* I said. I didn't want to deal with the hassle of operating a business, nor did I want to manage a staff. I didn't want to deal with the issues of staff benefits, insurance, or make other general employment decisions.

Fear then turned into doubt. They go hand-in-hand and are like close cousins that you always see together. Not only did I tell myself I never *wanted* to open a law practice, but I also told myself I couldn't. Fear and doubt were working hard on their jobs in my mind. Their mission is to lie and make us lose sight of who we are. If we allow them, they will accomplish their mission.

When it came to opening my law office, my mind continuously went back and forth with the idea of being a business owner. Mental

The Strength to Conquer Fear

gymnastics were required to convince myself that opening a practice was the best choice for me. Overcoming my fears led me to thinking beyond the challenges that caused me to be filled with doubt. I wanted to find new ways to live my best life.

Although my government job provided a stable career, competitive salary and benefits, great health insurance, and a flexible schedule, I wanted the liberty to be more available to the needs of my growing family, without having to answer to anyone. Starting my own law practice would also give me the autonomy and authority to choose the cases on which I wanted to work. In addition, I'd no longer have to be concerned about salary ceilings or waiting for someone else to promote me. I could promote myself.

My "truth" was I wanted to start a law firm, but I talked myself out of it before it even became a possibility. Have you ever done that? Have you ever talked yourself out of something because you were too afraid of what could happen? Maybe you didn't have to convince yourself not to do it. You may have stopped at the thought itself. Fear has the power to suppress our thoughts and our desire to speak of our goals. It has the ability to prevent us from stepping onto the path of success if we allow it.

Each of us must discover our own truth. Once we discover our truth, we can't let fear and doubt overshadow it. When fear captures our minds and takes us hostage, we must remember *"with God all things are possible."*

Fear tells us we are comfortable where we are, and there is no need for change. In my early twenties all I dreamed of was the day I could be comfortable and enjoy the fruits of my labor. It had taken so much time and energy to get to a comfortable place in my career, and I was finally coasting. In my finite mind, I thought I'd surely reached my ceiling—attained my reward. However, I hadn't even scratched the surface.

Comfort can hinder our ability to reach the highest of heights. The greatest accomplishments in society were not achieved in comfort zones.

They were achieved when people pushed the limit. Media giant Oprah Winfrey might never have reached the level of fame and influence she has today if she had been content with only hosting a local television show. Had she remained comfortable where she began—actress, philanthropist, producer, and network owner are titles she might never have held.

Limiting Fear

Fear limits us. It always gives us the "dismal failure" ending when the ultimate failure is allowing fear to stop us from moving in the first place. Fear delayed my writing this book for nearly five years. Every year I had one excuse after another. Every time I began writing, I experienced fear and self-doubt.

"Who wants to read about my life?"

"Who am I to write a book?"

Not only did these questions swirl around in my head, but I spoke them. It is important we speak truth to power. Remember, words are powerful, and they impact our lives.

I'm sure my husband got tired of hearing and responding to the same old questions. Nevertheless, he continued to encourage me.

"April, some young girl needs to hear your story."

Many times, my husband's words of encouragement were exactly what I needed to write one more paragraph. His encouragement helped the fear subside a little more each time.

We all need at least one person to be our "cheerleader". We can benefit from having someone in our corner to help drive the fear away. We should surround ourselves with people who see our vision and who can help us navigate through the fog of fear and doubt. We need people who will remind us of our purpose.

As a teenage mother, fear led me to think I could not pursue my dreams with a child. I could have listened, but I chose not to. I could have listened when it told me I didn't have the resources to start a law practice. Fear also could have prevented this book from becoming a reality, all while it remained in Google Drive for many more years. Thank God I did not listen.

Thank God I listened to the Holy Spirit reminding me I have the power to win. I'm not the only one who possesses this power. You have the power too!

Conquering Fear

When staring fear in the face ask yourself, *"What do I truly want?"* Then ask, *"What is the alternative?"*

I knew I wanted to go college. I wanted the opportunity to choose a career that I'd love. I didn't want to be forced into a job because I needed to make ends meet. That was my only alternative. The alternative was not to pursue my goals, but to remain home and find a job that would support me and my child. It wasn't what I wanted. It wasn't what I was going to love. Many times, our alternative leads us to doing just that—not pursuing a path we love.

Continuing my federal career was the alternative to opening a law practice. Although it was still a great option, it was not my destination. It was only a rest stop along my journey. Had I remained in that job position, I would've easily become complacent and comfortable too soon in my career.

In the place of fear, God has blessed us with a sound mind. Making sound decisions can help drive fear away. It is not necessary to make the riskiest move to conquer fear. It can be done gradually. Remember, conquering fear is a process. It is conquered by simply deciding to make *a* move. Take the first step. Write the first word. Make the first call. Whatever your move consists of, Do It!

After I became pregnant, enrolling into college was the first move I made to conquer my fear of allowing the words of others to determine my future. Discussing with my husband my goal of starting a law practice was the first step to help me crush my fear of leaving a stable career with the federal government. Continuing to write was the small step I took to overcome my fear of sharing this book with the world. Again, the steps we need to make to conquer fear don't have to be the biggest steps.

Just Move

An illustration I think of is how fear can prevent you from driving to your desired destination. It would be conquered by allowing yourself to first walk to the vehicle. (1. Taking the initial step). The process continues by sitting in the driver's seat. (2. Placing yourself in a position of power). Before starting the ignition, it is necessary to perform the necessary safety checks. (3. Evaluate the situation carefully. Don't forget your seatbelt!). Starting the ignition and gently placing your foot on the pedal is your final step. (4. Activate your strength). Conquering fear doesn't mean you have to arrive quickly. Driving the speed limit, or even a little under, is okay—

just move.

As with driving to any destination you may encounter a roadblock that will cause you to carefully consider your next move. That's okay. Detours are a part of the journey. When you face an obstacle, just remember to ask yourself, *"What is my alternative?"* What can I expect if I do not move at all? If your alternative is not what you desire for your life, or if it requires you to give up on your dreams and goals, do not stop. That is your signal to keep moving.

4

STRONG FAITH

"He replied, "Because you have so little faith. Truly I tell you, if you have faith as small as a mustard seed, you can say to this mountain, 'Move from here to there,' and it will move. Nothing will be impossible for you."

Matthew 17:20

I have friends who tell me they learned to drive at thirteen and fourteen years old.

Only the Strong Thrive

Some learned even earlier. Driving was second nature and came easily to them. Not for me. Learning to drive was one of my most dreadful and difficult learning experiences. It took a while for me to get the hang of it.

It was so difficult because many of my first lessons were taught using a stick shift. I could never gauge the right time to place my foot on the clutch, move the gear knob, and press the gas. It was too much going on at once. After many failed lessons, I gave up hope on ever being able to drive a stick shift.

I can't blame my lack of driving skills all on the stick shift though. Driving an automatic did not come easily either. It took three driving tests before I passed, and I had an accident the first day driving to school. To say learning to drive was a bad experience would be an understatement.

Most parents are a little uneasy when their children get close to driving age. I was more than uneasy when my son became old enough to learn to drive. I was terrified. I thought his driving experience would be like mine. He asked several times over, "*When are you going to let me drive?*" and I always found some excuse why it wasn't time.

Though I knew I'd have to deal with reality at some point, I waited as long as I could before teaching him. I finally gave in one night while we happened to be the only car left in an empty parking lot. I was pleasantly surprised during our first lesson. He wasn't nearly as bad as I was, and he showed great progress with each lesson.

However, I was still nervous for him to become a full-time driver. I was so nervous, I followed right behind him on his first day driving to school. If I'd never had to activate my faith before this experience, I truly had to in that moment.

I had no control as he cranked his car and pulled out of our driveway. I had to believe the hours of practice and the safe driving skills he'd learned with me and in drivers' education would govern his driving habits. However, my trust in his skills didn't mean I could trust how others would drive, and it didn't calm my nerves much more. To totally release my fear, I had to rely on faith that God would cover and protect him on the roadways throughout the day.

Faith works in many ways. In situations where we have no control, we can engage our faith through preparation, prayer, and trust that God will safely guard us—similar to releasing my teenage driver on the roadways. I had prepared him and given him the tools he needed to safely travel. There was not much more preparation I could have provided when he traveled on the road. I had to believe he was protected by my prayers that he and others would drive carefully. I had to rely on my faith in knowing God had the power to keep him safe.

We can engage our faith in other ways too. When we want to achieve a goal, we can't only prepare and pray about it. We must make a move! We can't say we trust God to get us to a destination when we have yet to take the first step. We can't get in the driver's seat like we discussed in the previous chapter and then just sit there. When we engage our faith in this way, we're all in—pedal to the metal. We can drive at the speed of a racecar because we know nothing is impossible.

At other times, we must activate our faith in a completely different way. In situations where we've done all we can, and we've exhausted all other options, relying on faith seems like the common-sense next step. We realize taking active measures won't help. There's no way we can prepare and taking steps on our own won't solve the problem.

In these situations, we have no choice but to trust God because there's nothing else we can do ourselves. When we realize there's nothing we can do, we must pray and engage our faith in what may be the most difficult way. In this way, we activate faith by not making a move at all. Our faith is revealed by being completely silent, still, and in trusting God to work it out.

A Small Faith Move

Before my pregnancy, I had been accepted into a college located miles away from home. I was excited and eager to add to the credit hours I'd already accumulated from my high school dual enrollment classes. But afterward, I knew it would not be feasible to begin my first semester of college miles away from home with my delivery date being so close. It was necessary to consider doing something I didn't want to do.

Instead of immediately pursuing the college of my choice, I reluctantly registered for classes at the local community college near my hometown. As I stood in line at the registrar's office, it became clear that my life would not take the course I'd planned. I felt defeated. I thought I'd failed before I even began. I didn't want to stay home and attend college. That was not my original plan! If I didn't attend my desired college right then, I might never be able to go, or so I thought.

Strong Faith

I gave birth to a sweet baby boy on a Sunday in August. I was proud to be his mother, and I enjoyed bonding with him after his birth. Nonetheless, my anxiety was overwhelming. Classes at the community college were beginning the very next day. I could not get out of the hospital fast enough.

Immediately after being discharged, we stopped by the college campus to make sure I had everything I needed to start classes. Thankfully, I was able to take distance learning courses that didn't require attendance on campus every day. Being a teenage mother was a new, difficult, and exhausting task alone. Adding a 15-hour course load complicated matters, but I stayed the course.

Though continuing my education so soon after giving birth to my son was a small move in exercising my faith, it was a step along my journey that helped to engage my faith in even more challenging situations.

When I decided to attend law school, I had

no clue how I was going to pay for it; where I was going to go; or how I would handle the demanding schedule with a child. Even though I did not readily have all the answers, I decided to take the required Law School Admissions Test (LSAT). Once I received my score I began applying to different schools.

I knew I wanted to remain in my home state. I wanted to be close to family with my child, but I also applied to schools out of state because I didn't want to limit my options. My first offer came from an out-of-state school. I didn't want to move that far from home, alone, with my son. I'd tried moving from home with him a few years before, and I ended up back at home because it was too difficult to manage. I certainly did not want to go down that road again.

But in faith, I decided I would move out of state. I still didn't know how I would pay for school or how I would handle childcare. I just made the decision to go. Shortly after I'd set my mind on moving, I received an acceptance letter from an in-state school. It wasn't just an acceptance letter either. It included a scholarship!

Strong Faith

On the one hand, I was a little uneasy because I had to commit to the school by a certain date to take advantage of the scholarship. I didn't want to be rushed into acceptance and likely be giving up opportunities at other schools. But on the other hand, the offer was everything I needed to satisfy my financial need and my desire to stay close to home. I could hear God say, "*Trust me.*"

So, in faith, I immediately responded to the letter and accepted the offer of admission into the school. I didn't wait for other offers to come. I didn't have to; I had everything I needed.

I try to keep this response and God's many other responses at the forefront of my mind, especially when I'm asked to make a "faith move" that I'm unsure about. Uncomfortable and challenging situations create the perfect space to allow our faith to work.

A Big Faith Move

Resigning from a career position with the federal government to start my law practice might have been one of the biggest faith moves I've made in my life. With every step I took, I know God was with me.

My husband and I had just welcomed our third child two months before I resigned. All I had to rely on was faith. I had no office space and no clients. I didn't have a business grant or loan to get me started. I only had a dream and the drive to make it work.

Don't get me wrong, I didn't just wake up one day and start a law practice. The year before, my husband and I started discussing and planning for it. I asked him what he thought about me resigning from my job to open a law office.

"I think that's a great idea!"

He said it with no hesitation. His words perked my ears and my heart.

We then discussed the ins and outs of what

resigning from my job would entail. We decided that we would have another baby before I would leave. One month after we made that decision, I became pregnant. We didn't expect it to happen that quickly, but I knew it was the answer to my prayer. It was as if God was saying, *"Okay, I've made my move, now make yours!"* From that day forward, my plan was put in motion.

We don't stop making faith moves when we reach a set goal or a desired place in life. Moving in faith should be our way of life. I'm still moving in faith as I make life, family, and career decisions. The need to activate our faith never ends, but I've found it easier to rely on God as I journey on this faith walk. He increases my faith every time He moves on my behalf in ways that I know no one else can.

Still Faith

One of the hardest moves of faith is the move we can't make at all. My family was recently in the midst of a devastating storm that was set to ruin years of hard work, and there was nothing I could do about it. If there is ever an issue with my children or with my husband, I always jump into "fix it" mode. I quickly learned that my strength alone will not always be able to protect them.

For a few days I ran around trying to fix the issue like I always do. I jumped into "mama-bear," investigator, and lawyer mode all at the same time—a damaging trio.

After a few days of running myself ragged, I decided it was not my problem to fix. *"I have to go to God with this one,"* I said to myself. In releasing it to my Father, I sat down and wrote this prayer:

Abba Father, thank you for the covenant that was sealed with Your Son's blood. You have offered us an intimate relationship with You. I want to be fully committed to being in Your presence. You have offered a relationship like none other. Show me how to take advantage of it in the best way. I am truly blessed. Help me to realize, understand, and remember the blessing is not in things but is in You and the chance to live intimately with You. Keep my focus there. Satan is all around, trying to destroy my family, our character, and our name. Lord but I know if we call on You, You can stop him with just one word, one thought. I know who holds all Power, and in that knowledge I rest and have peace. Lord just tell me what You want us to do before You will move. Increase our faith, Father. I know You love us and don't want any harm to come our way. Your awesome Strength and Power is all we need. It is more than we need, Lord. Thank You for the unfailing love You've shown by giving us Jesus. We did not deserve Him but You loved us just that much. What is man that you are mindful of us? Your love, grace, and mercy are more than we deserve, and we thank You for them. Lead me and guide me in the ways that You want Father so that I can serve You. Take away any thoughts or activities that will hinder my service to You. Give us the victory in the end! In Jesus' Holy name. Amen.

A peace came over me after my prayer. While lying in bed that night, my husband and I resolved that neither of us would worry any longer about it. We wouldn't even speak on it. We had turned it over to God. We slept well that night.

Around noon the very next day, my husband called to tell me the issue I'd been running myself ragged to try to "handle" had been resolved. I couldn't believe it! Yet, at the same time I could. I know this is how God works. I'd seen Him work in the same way many times before. I scolded myself for trying to handle it on my own. Why didn't I take it to Him first?

We will encounter moments of difficulty on our faith journey. Our human response is to use our own strength, our own minds, and our own abilities to get the results we want. However, we limit God's blessings when we fail to engage our faith. We have not because we ask not. We shouldn't be afraid to take every problem, every issue, and even every dream and aspiration to God. We should take it all to Him first.

Strong Faith

Living by faith doesn't mean we know that God will certainly do everything we request. Faith is in knowing He can. We don't know how He will answer prayers, but our faith is in knowing that His answers are what He sees best for our lives. His will for us sometimes seems confusing and perplexing, but we can be confident knowing we're on the right path no matter the bumps, turns, or roadblocks along the way.

5

THE STRENGTH TO FOCUS

"Let your eyes look straight ahead; fix your gaze directly before you. Give careful thought to the paths for your feet and be steadfast in all your ways."

Proverbs 4:25-26

I have a lot of trouble with my eyesight. In the fifth grade my teacher recognized I had

The Strength to Focus

problems seeing the chalkboard. I had a significant squint. It didn't matter how close I stood to the chalkboard, I still needed to squint. It was the only way I could see, but for some reason she was the first person to point it out and suggest I go see a doctor. *I* didn't even realize I had limitations.

My mom finally took me to an optometrist who prescribed glasses. Because we didn't have private vision insurance, I didn't have much of a choice in the design I wanted for my glasses. I had to get Medicaid-approved glasses, which meant I would have to choose from the least desirable frames in the office. The frames were brown in color and were thicker than any frames I could have imagined. I didn't want to wear them. I knew they would make me the laughingstock of my class, so I hesitantly placed them on my face. When I walked outside with my new glasses on, there was clarity like I'd never seen.

With my glasses, I no longer had to squint. I didn't see everything as a jumbled blur. Out of all the newness I could now see, the thing that shocked me most was how beautiful the tall trees were. Beforehand the tops of the tall trees looked like one giant green ball. I could now look up high and see that the trees were made up of individual leaves and that each leaf had its own separate and distinct shape. As pleasant as it was, it was at the same time disheartening to know I'd lived so many years in a complete blur, thinking that was just the way things were. I was disappointed that I'd walked around every day missing nature's true beauty.

I couldn't focus and thrive in class when my eyesight wasn't clear. The same is true in life. It's difficult to thrive when our vision isn't clear. We can't focus on a goal that we haven't identified or set our sights on. The best way to identify our goals is to first know what our hearts truly desire.

Sometimes identifying our goals or desires is the hardest part. Many things can make it difficult. As we've discussed in previous chapters, many times we don't think we're good enough to accomplish a certain goal. Other times, fear comes in and blocks our hearts. We look at the task ahead and believe it's going to be too hard. We think we don't have enough resources. We wonder what will happen if we start down the road and can't complete the journey.

We can't limit ourselves though. The sky is not the limit anymore. There are *no* limits! Don't set boundaries on your heart when your options are limitless.

Once we've set our minds, our thoughts, words, and actions must follow in line. The straighter the line, the easier it is to focus. The longer these things are in sync with one another, the more we begin to see the progress we've made toward our goals. Our vision becomes clearer. Be cautious, though. No matter how clear our vision becomes, if we get distracted or place other things before our goals, our vision will become blurred again.

Laser Focus

At one point in my life, it became very easy to keep a laser focus on my desired goals. I wasn't easily distracted. I couldn't put energy into anything that would blur my focus. It was important for me to set boundaries and let people know where my focus lay. Setting those boundaries made it almost impossible for anyone to come into my space and get me off track. Not that they didn't try. I just wasn't having it at the time.

When I was in law school, I had to keep a laser focus on school. I was in a pretty serious relationship, but there were several times when I had to "lay down the law" with my husband, who was my boyfriend at the time. Many days he wanted to hang out or do things that would interfere with my studying, but I had to remind him where my focus was at that time.

Spending time with him became almost non-existent due to my demanding schedule. He'd also get tired of my books tagging along with us nearly everywhere we went. We argued about it, and at times, I didn't think our relationship would survive. Honestly, that was a risk I was willing to take. It took a lot of strength to risk love and companionship for my dreams. Not that I didn't love or care for him, but I needed him to understand the struggles I'd gone through to get to this point. I couldn't just throw it all away.

My focus wasn't always as strong as it was in law school. In fact, it wasn't nearly as strong as it should have been, especially while I was in high school. I didn't realize it at the time but reading through the journal I'd kept all those years opened my eyes. Re-visiting that time period showed me how I allowed distractions to get me off track.

For quite some time, I hadn't written a word in the journal about what I wanted for my future or my plans for college. However, I wrote a lot about the things that distracted me. Hanging out on the weekends and partying with friends became important to me. Not only was my focus not in the right place, but I also saw that I placed myself in situations that thwarted progress towards my goals. I plainly disregarded my own advice and let my physical eyes take control over my mind, thoughts, and actions. When describing a guy I liked in the journal I wrote, "I have feelings for him and care for him, but I don't think I would marry him. I don't think he's the right one anyway. He does some things that I don't agree with."

Instead of listening to myself, focusing on school and preparing for college, I decided to continue on a path that would keep me distracted for years. I set myself back by taking my eyes off my desired goals. It's easy to do. Think about a time you were distracted. It may have taken years to get back on track.

Relationship with God

The best way to get back on track is to first nurture our relationship with God. I realize now that each time my focus was misplaced, I was focused more on nurturing my relationships with other people: my family, my boyfriend, my friends, or my classmates. It wasn't until my first year of law school that I truly started to nurture my relationship with God, and it wasn't something I deliberately set out to do. I *had* to.

The Strength to Focus

The first year broke me down in so many ways that I had no choice but to call on Him. I was hundreds of miles from my son and the rest of my family. My boyfriend and I were in a rocky, long distance relationship. The stress of maintaining a long-distance relationship, the feelings of loneliness, and the rigorous coursework weren't the best combination for my mental state.

One night as I was sitting in bed, with the Bible on one side of me and a constitutional law book on the other, I let out a loud cry. I cried out to God for mental and spiritual healing. This wasn't a couple of seconds with a few tears running down my face type of cry either. This was a full-heart, full-spirit, and full-body cry. It was a cry for clarity. The loneliness, exhaustion, and confusion had gotten the best of me. I needed to know if it was all worth it.

In the midst of my cry, I felt God's Spirit comforting me. I heard, *"I am with you. I will never leave you."* In between sobs of cry, I told God that if He got me through this trying time, I was going to live like it. I was going to put Him first.

Only the Strong Thrive

Once I'd decided that I was going to let God be the center of my life, my focus became so much clearer. Dedication and determination paved the way for me to reach my goals. My intelligence, education, and skill-set could only take me part of the way, but a focused mind with dedication and determination could take me over the finish line.

Dedication is being committed to a task or a purpose. People sometimes use the word grind. Dedication is the same thing. It's a grind; a loyal commitment. Every move we make—whether it's in our teens, 20s, 30s or beyond—must be intentional and purposeful in order to get us to our desired destination.

Determination is similar. It's making a firm decision and being resolved not to change it. It's telling ourselves and the world that we will not stop, no matter what comes our way.

Many times, the road became too hard to travel, and I wanted to give up. I could have easily let it all go. It would have been easier to quit. But because my focus was in the right place, I was able to see that my thoughts of quitting were nothing but distractions, too.

We may never completely master the art of keeping our focus in the right place. It's the same as many of our other life-long projects. We continue to work and practice at it. I still struggle, as most of us probably do, when the whirlwind of life happens. I sometimes get so caught up in the day to day—getting the kids to school, cooking, cleaning, working, and every other little thing that's going on that I lose focus on God. I've found myself nurturing my relationship with everyone else and neglecting my relationship with God. When I realize this is happening, I immediately have a miniature version of my first year of law school "Come to Jesus" moment, and I get myself back together.

Never too Late

We are focused most when our actions line up with our end goal. Each time I engaged in meaningless activities on my journey, I was ultimately adding more time to reaching my goals. I wish I had been better focused when I was younger, but I'm thankful for second and third chances.

You may think it's too late to focus on your goals. Your children may be teenagers or in college; one of your past plans may have fallen through; or you may feel like your finances are holding you back. But it's never too late.

Just like it's never too late to get glasses for clearer vision, it's never too late to discover your vision. In fact, I know people who never needed glasses until they got older. It was the perfect time to get them.

Each of our visions and goals will look different. For me, becoming an attorney was part of mine. I knew my goals would require many more years of school after high school. Your goals and visions may not include going to a professional school like mine. It doesn't have to include school at all. Allow your passions to help pave your avenues, escort and guide you to the

The Strength to Focus

life God has designed just for you.

There are no requirements to the dreams you dream, the visions you see, or the goals you set. They need only be what your heart truly desires and what you are willing to work for.

6

THE STRENGTH TO FORGIVE AND BE FREE

"Bear with each other and forgive one another if any of you has a grievance against someone. Forgive as the Lord forgave you."

Colossians 3:13

Many years ago, I got a tattoo of a butterfly that covers a sizeable portion of my upper arm. I'm in the process of having it removed, finally. I've been wanting to have it removed for some time, but the removal process

The Strength to Forgive and Be Free

intimidated me.

I loved the tattoo when I first got it at eighteen years old. At the time, I thought it was the cool thing to do. Many of my friends had tattoos and I felt like I needed one too. One day, after having it for several years, the tattoo I once loved so much didn't appeal to me anymore. I guess you could say I'd grown out of it. The people I once hung out with weren't around. I had moved away from home and was in a different place in my life. The tattoo reminded me of a time I didn't want to re-live and, as a result, I began wearing shirts that would cover it up.

In all honesty, the tattoo removal process is not the most pleasant experience. So far, I've had multiple laser treatments performed by a trained dermatologist. Although it's a painful procedure, I've seen more and more of the tattoo removed after each treatment. It's been quite mind-blowing to see the changes.

Once the process is complete, my arms will be free! Sleeveless shirts will no longer hang in the back of my closet. Of course, I'll never forget the tattoo that was once there, but I won't have to be reminded of the unpleasant moments in my life every time I look at my arm. I will no longer have to go to great lengths to cover it up. The tattoo won't hold me back anymore.

Forgiveness is much like my tattoo removal. It may not be the most pleasant process. We may never forget what caused the pain, but the pain no longer holds us back.

A Complicated Process

Although forgiveness can be a multi-layered, complex, and sometimes painful process, it is a key requirement to living an abundant and thriving life. Its complex and intertwined pieces must come together to gain true freedom, peace of mind, and a settled spirit.

Forgiveness is complicated because it doesn't come naturally. It is a process that is learned and must be intentionally worked through. As soon as children hit the toddler stage, parents and other adults have to teach them how to interact with peers who have upset them. Many times, those lessons have been taught over and over, especially if a child is upset that a peer has taken away a favored toy. That child's natural response is to hold on to it. Our response is the same. If someone has hurt us, it is not the easiest thing to let go. Their actions may have caused devastating pain and scarred us.

Forgiveness is also complicated and multi-layered because the process may require forgiving several people, including ourselves. Sometimes we blame ourselves for someone else's actions. Other times, we feel guilty for even allowing them to hurt us in the first place.

Forgiveness requires us to be open and honest. It forces us to share our inner-most feelings which can make us feel vulnerable. Forgiveness unmasks emotions and holds people accountable.

Like my tattoo removal, professional help may be needed to assist in the process. Each step of forgiveness may not be completed at the same time either. It may take years before it's complete. The time it takes, the complexity, and the people involved may intimidate and prevent us from engaging in the process, but we must do it. Holding on to the hurt, pain, neglect, and suffering keeps us from living a fulfilled life.

A Never-Ending Nightmare

For years I secretly held on to the hurt and pain that began when I was seven years old. What seemed like a harmless overnight visit by a trusted family member turned into a nightmare. While asleep in the beautiful canopy bed that I loved so much, I was awakened by a feeling I had never felt before.

Initially, I was a bit dazed and confused by what was going on. I'd never felt anything like it. As I became fully awake, I sat up. He put his hand to my mouth. *"Shh,"* he said while pushing me back down. I had no choice but to comply.

As I lay there in the dark with my eyes open looking up toward the ceiling, many thoughts bombarded me. I knew this was all wrong. Here was this much older man lying beside my bed, painfully touching me in areas I had never been touched before. I did not know what to do.

As he got up and left my room, I thought for sure that was the end of it all, but I was wrong. That would be the first of many encounters of sexual abuse and molestation at his hand. I was too afraid to tell anyone, especially my dad.

My dad had a very short and fiery temper. I knew this because I had a front seat view of the fighting between him and my mom. Also, at one point I saw him pull a different family member out of our car and put a gun to their head, while my brothers and I cried, *"Don't do it!"* from the back seat.

I knew that if I said anything, my abuser would not only stop coming to my room, he would be

Only the Strong Thrive

dead. I didn't want his blood on my hands. And I didn't want my father in prison for the rest of his life.

For a very long time, I kept it to myself. Over a period of about seven years I continued to be victimized over and over again. I hated being home or at a family member's house alone because I knew he could show up at any time.

One day when my dad was at work and my brothers were outside playing, the door eerily opened. My heart fell out of my chest. I knew it was him. Just a few days before, he had come by and forced me to engage in the same demoralizing acts as he did every other time he caught me alone. Each time I thought I had the courage to stop him, but I didn't. Each time I'd prepare myself and say, *"I'm not doing this anymore."* Yet, I never had the strength to stop him.

But on this day, I'd had enough.

He came into our house and immediately started touching me. I was terrified! My first response was to run. I ran to my brother's room.

The Strength to Forgive and Be Free

He chased me and threw me on the bed. My fright then turned to anger. I fought with all my might, pushed him off, and slid from underneath him. I ran. He continued behind me. I gasped for air as my energy began to drain. It felt like we ran around the house for an hour. I was exhausted.

At some point he threw me on the wall, grabbed and sucked on my neck while choking me. Somehow, I got away.

"He's going to kill me! I have to fight back," I thought.

It was then that I knew I had to do something. I was no longer going to be the victim. I was not going to allow him to force me to do things I didn't want to do. I'd hoped the abuse would eventually stop or that someone would protect me, but protection never came. I had to protect myself from further abuse, no matter the cost. I freed myself from his grip, ran to the kitchen, and grabbed the biggest knife I could find. I put it to his neck and looked sternly at him with my lips clenched tight.

"If you ever touch me again, I will kill you!"

I said those words. I *meant* those words. Wow, I was stronger than I thought!

The Aftermath

That was the last day he ever touched me. It was the last day I suffered direct and physical abuse at his hands. However, the emotional and mental trauma continued.

I tried to hide the memories far in the back of my mind. I was working and pushing hard to reach my goals. I couldn't dwell on the past. But there were times when he'd call and attempt to converse with me like he had not caused devastation and heartache for most of my childhood.

He even called while I was in my last year of law school to ask me to testify on his behalf to get him out of prison, for an unrelated crime. I thought, how dare he? The audacity! Nonetheless, something in my heart struggled with the idea of saying no. To this day, I still don't understand why. It was almost as if I valued his life more than I valued mine.

Even at a younger age, I wanted to protect his life. It was compassion in the most distorted way. Thankfully his hearing was set for the day before I was due to have my second child. I wouldn't have been able to go anyway. God gave me a graceful way out.

Being sexually abused for most of my childhood affected my life in more ways than one. Sexual abuse is known to cause lasting consequences. Teenagers who have been sexually abused as children are at increased risk for becoming pregnant. Sexual abuse often leads to depression, post-traumatic stress disorder, loss of trust, an altered perception about sexual behavior, and the propensity to be further victimized throughout adulthood. I was never counseled nor diagnosed, but I silently suffered with many of the effects of sexual abuse.

I certainly had an altered perception about

sexual behavior. I engaged in behaviors like the actions forced upon me for all those years, and I became pregnant before graduating from high school. I was no saint. However, during that time, I didn't realize my behaviors might have been connected to the abuse I suffered.

I've always had a difficult time with trust as well. I am a very guarded person, and I've been reluctant to let my guard down since childhood. My husband can attest to that. He fought hard for years to get me to open up to him. Looking back, I wish I had gotten the professional help I needed. I am still a work in progress.

A Recipe for Disaster

At some point I learned I was not my abuser's only victim. He was able to smoothly maneuver between many other homes with young children. The news broke my heart, although I wasn't surprised. I was surprised, however, that no one was able to prevent the abuse. I wondered if there were other ways we could've been protected.

As a society, we may never fully know or understand why certain people have the propensity to engage in abusive behaviors, especially against children. However, as adults, we must do what we can to prevent children from suffering years of abuse in silence.

In hindsight, I believe I continued to be a victim of abuse because my brothers and I were left home alone so often. In the midst of the complex and troubling life circumstances, we were not monitored as carefully as we should have been. Our parents and other adults were distracted by other things.

I was also not educated about improper sexual behavior and the safe ways to report it. I might have felt more comfortable revealing the abuse to a caring adult who asked specific questions about whether I'd ever been improperly touched. Knowing active measures would've been immediately taken to prevent further abuse, and also knowing I wouldn't have been ridiculed, embarrassed, or shamed might've helped ease my fears about reporting the abuse. However, I didn't have those assurances at that time.

Observant adults, education, and safe reporting procedures may not eliminate childhood sexual abuse altogether, but I believe they are positive actions and efforts that might save a child from a lifetime of suffering.

Revealing the Secret

More than 15 years after I put a knife to my abuser's neck, I finally revealed the secret to my parents. I'd been holding it inside for years. It's not uncommon for victims of sexual abuse to do the same.

Recently, there's been a wave of women who have garnered national attention after exposing high profile men who have sexually violated them. The first thing most people ask when questioning the testimony of these women is, *"Why'd they wait so long to reveal this?"* That's a question I can answer. I'm sure they have their own reasons, as I had mine.

The Strength to Forgive and Be Free

I felt ashamed and embarrassed. I didn't know what my parents' response would be. Would they even believe me? I assumed if I dealt with it myself, it would be one less issue in my family. We had already gone through so much—the separation and divorce of my parents, my dad's incarceration, and the day to day struggles of my single-father dad raising four children. What young girl would really want to add to that?

Now, however, the things that were once concerns were no longer my concern when the time came for me to reveal what happened to me. I now had a greater concern. I had a bigger reason to reveal it. I had a daughter of my own, and I had to protect her. She was two years old at the time and had been occasionally visiting family back in my hometown.

Although it was very unlikely my daughter would encounter him, I felt it necessary to caution my mom and to explain why I was so guarded about her visits. There had also been some family talk about why I was so guarded and would not allow my daughter to go to certain places. So, it made sense to reveal it.

Only the Strong Thrive

I called my mom. Yet again I was calling her to break devastating news. To say she was shocked is an understatement. She immediately wanted me to call my dad. It felt like déjà vu. Years earlier, my dad said the same words to me in response to me revealing my teenage pregnancy to him— "*Call your mom.*" Only now, my relationship with my mom was significantly stronger than it was years before.

I felt nearly the same about calling my dad as I had felt about calling my mom back then. I didn't want to do it. I was 30 years old, married with children and living my own life, but there was still hesitancy about calling him. I could not predict what he would do. My mother wasn't going to let me off the hook though, so we called him together.

He was devastated and an emotional wreck. He couldn't believe it. He blamed himself. He thought maintaining custody of me after he and my mom separated would've prevented the likelihood of me being sexually abused. He wanted to watch and to protect me, and to be careful of whom he allowed me to hang around. He thought he had failed.

He called me one day shortly after that phone call. He was not coping well with the thought of one day seeing the man who stole his daughter's innocence. It was difficult for my dad even to say his name. He asked me how I thought he should handle it.

"Forgive him and love him like Jesus loves him."

Those words rolled off my tongue so easily. Despite the torture, the pain, and the shame I carried around for so long, I'd had the strength to let it all go. I wanted so badly for my dad to be able to let it go, too. I'd hoped *my* peace would give *him* peace.

Closure

The peace that came after I revealed the abuse to my parents was the final layer I needed to complete my forgiveness process. Sharing our pain with others is a positive step in the right direction. It is difficult to recover from the hurt we've endured when we haven't shared our thoughts and feelings with those closest to us.

In addition to sharing our feelings, we must also relinquish our need for an apology. Many people do not find peace because they feel they need an apology first. However, forgiveness can't be locked away and reserved for apologies only. That may never happen.

The purest form of forgiveness is that which is done freely, without request. Through strength, I freed myself from the bondage of my own unforgiving heart. I knew I couldn't thrive with that heavy weight resting on me and my spirit. It would have held me down. The past wrongs, hurts, and failures would have consumed me. With those burdens, I would not have been able to truly enjoy the blessings and fruits of life.

I've been in the same setting with my abuser a few times over the years. While it was uncomfortable at times, I always tried to be polite. Several years after I opened up to my parents, he reached out to me again. A Facebook message popped up from him. I saw his name and stared at my phone before deciding whether to open it.

"I'm sorry for what I did."

Were my eyes deceiving me? I couldn't believe what I was reading. I never expected an apology. I can't say I even wanted one. I could have continued through life without it. I had already given myself permission to walk in freedom. I didn't need his apology to be free.

But reading those words did something else for me. Imagine what it would feel like, not only to stretch your wings, but to fly.

For years he tried to carry on with me the same as he did with everyone else, acting as if he hadn't caused much distress in my childhood. His apology was acceptance. It was a confession. He was admitting that he had abused me, and I felt vindicated.

For me, admitting he had abused me was more significant than "sorry." He didn't need to lay out his transgressions word for word. Those few words were enough. Nothing he could have said would've changed my heart. I had already chosen to forgive him.

"I forgave you a long time ago," I replied.

If nothing else, I'd hoped my words somehow freed him too.

7

THE STRENGTH TO LOVE

"Love bears all things, believes all things, hopes all things, endures all things."

I Corinthians 13:7

"Mom, why do you love him so bad?" my three-year-old asked as she watched me, for the millionth time, tightly hug her little brother and land multiple kisses on his cheek.

Only the Strong Thrive

With a confused look on my face, I chuckled.

"Why do I love him so bad?"

She looked at me and smiled. *"Well,"* as she smacked her lips. *"Why do you love him so good?"*

"I love you so bad, too," I said laughing. *"Come here and let me show you!"*

My three-year-old has her own perception of what love means. We all do. To her, love is wrapped up in the tight kisses and hugs I give. Many times we think of love in those ways too: the hugs, the kisses, and the "I love you's." For someone who doesn't remember many hugs, kisses, or "I love you's" growing up, I think it is important to express our love in those ways. It feels good. It provides a sense of comfort. However, the "truest" form of love does not necessarily manifest itself in those ways.

When we measure love based solely on feelings, we overlook its steadfastness, its power and its strength. We place it on shaky and unreliable ground. If feelings defined love, some of us would be loved today and not tomorrow. We would be loved one second and not loved the next. Love is more stable than that. Love doesn't always feel.

Love acts.

An Act of Love

The most profound characterization of love is given in I Corinthians 13.

"Love is patient, love is kind. It does not envy, it does not boast, it is not proud. It does not dishonor others, it is not self-seeking, it is not easily angered, it keeps no record of wrongs. Love does not delight in evil but rejoices with the truth. It always protects, always trusts, always hopes, always perseveres. Love never fails."

Love doesn't keep score of the good or the bad. It doesn't count someone out because they have failed too many times. It doesn't throw in the towel when all hope seems lost.

We sometimes do.

Going back to your childhood and beyond, who would you say loved you unconditionally? Who loved you even when your bad outweighed your good? In adulthood, many of us realize our first answer is our Heavenly Father. I am so thankful His love isn't conditioned on who we are or what we have done. Isn't it comforting to know His love doesn't keep record of our wrongs?

Other than God, who has loved you - no strings attached? For most people, it was probably their mother. Our mothers are the first to love us. We most often learn how to love by the love they have shown to us. For some time, it would have been tough for me to answer that question the same way most people would.

My mom left our family when I was nine years old, and she wasn't around much after that. There was a brief period when my father

The Strength to Love

was incarcerated that my brothers and I moved in with her. But that didn't last long for me. Shortly thereafter, I moved in with my grandmother.

It was hard growing up without my mother to teach and guide me, especially in relation to female things. Not surprisingly, at some point in my adolescent years, nature took its course. And when it did, and other "womanly" matters came along, I pretty much had to wing it.

One such time came when I was around 12 years old. A training bra was long overdue. I was tired of the stares, whispers, and laughs from the boys in my class. It was time to take matters into my own hands. When my granddad picked me up from softball practice one evening I asked him to take me to Wal-Mart to get "something".

While driving there, he asked, *"What do you need from Wal-Mart?"*

Nervous and uncomfortable, I mumbled, *"A training bra."*

He didn't say anything else. He probably was

just as uncomfortable as I was. Nevertheless, he continued on. When we got there, he walked around the aisles while I tried to figure out what I should be getting. I had no idea what I was looking for and neither did he. Ashamed, but not wanting him to know I didn't have a clue what I was doing, I picked up the first thing I saw that said, "training bra" and rushed to the register.

It was a somber ride home.

On days like that, I felt the greatest effects of not having my mom around. I always felt a sense of abandonment and loneliness when she left, but it seemed to slap me right in the face in those moments. What was wrong with me that she had to leave? What did I do that I now have to figure this stuff out on my own? I always connected her actions, or lack thereof, to my worth. Because she left, I was not worthy of love.

I didn't consider her reasons for leaving. At that age, I wouldn't have understood. All I knew was that she wasn't there when I needed her. A mother's love and guidance are vital to her child's development, especially her teenage daughter's. Her ears would have listened. Her shoulder would have pillowed many tears.

For an essay in my twelfth grade English class I wrote, "This situation has ruined me from living a normal life, ruined me emotionally. Anger, hurt, and pain have conquered me, even though I don't show it. I am angry because for ten years I have missed out on a true mother/daughter relationship."

I just didn't understand it. My friends' moms were present in their lives. I saw how dynamic their relationships were. I longed for that. I was broken and empty. But, thankfully not forever. The strength of love finally rushed in, filled my emptiness, and mended my broken heart.

Love Never Fails

Love never gives up. After I became pregnant in the twelfth grade, my relationship with my mom changed drastically. First and foremost, she was more present. Despite me not following her initial recommendation to have an abortion, she was there with me every step of the way after I revealed my pregnancy and after my son was born. She was there for every big and small moment that came thereafter. She became a foundation on which I could stand through the challenges and the triumphs.

I don't know if a light came on for her when she realized her only daughter was about to become a mother. Maybe it was the fact that she was becoming a grandmother. It could have been because she was in a better place and a more emotionally and mentally stable space. I didn't have the answers. What was evident was that she now had more time to devote to building our relationship. I never asked her the reasons why. It didn't matter.

Letting go of the feelings of abandonment, loneliness, and all of the other emotions I harbored over those years wasn't easy. Honestly it may have been easier to keep trekking on the path we had been on. I was nearly an adult. She had already missed so much. I didn't *need* her anymore, I thought. Many people in my shoes probably would've had the same thoughts. Our feelings and selfish desires can get in the way of letting love, *love*.

Love sees the best in people, and it wants the best for them. My thoughts could not have been only about myself during our reconciliation period; they had to be for my child as well. If his grandmother wanted to have a relationship with him, he deserved to have that relationship. Regardless of my feelings, I couldn't have selfishly withheld a grandmother's love from him. My feelings weren't important. The relationships were.

As a naïve and inexperienced teenager, I could have completely blocked the overflow of love and support that I've so richly possessed since rekindling the relationship with my mother. The abundance of blessings gained by our relationship has far surpassed any negative feelings of anger, hurt, or resentment that I felt for those years. Love didn't only give me a new outlook on life, it gave me a new life altogether. It softened my heart. It made all the difference in my life – through one relationship.

God's Love

I may have learned the importance of familial relationships from my dad who took in my youngest brother when he was just a baby. My mom gave birth to him sometime after she and my dad separated, but my dad raised him with us and treated him like his own child. I believe he actually treated him better.

I can't imagine the whispers and strange looks he probably got, but that didn't stop him from doing what he thought was best. He gave our little brother the chance to grow up in a home with his siblings instead of in a home where he would've been alone as the only child. I think of my husband's act of love in the same way. Although our oldest isn't his biological child, his love for him transcends their genetic relationship. That kind of love is strong.

A mother's love is just as strong. My love for my son yearned to guard him from a broken relationship with his grandmother so soon in his life. I wanted to shield him from years of questions and confusion. But as powerful as my love was for him, it in no way compares to God's love for him and God's love for us. His love has protected and covered us over and over.

We experience hard times, and we have our fair share of heartbreak, but God is always there to mend us and put us back together again. He's always there to welcome us back when we've strayed away.

I grew up in the church, but I didn't truly know the depth of God's love until later in life. It took some time, circumstances, growth, and wisdom to truly understand it. Much of what I learned from my early church experience was what would happen when I messed up. I knew about God's wrath, judgment, and damnation. I was scared into obedience. I didn't know or hear as much about God's love, grace, and mercy.

Even though I didn't understand the magnitude of God's character, I look back and know He was ordering my steps even then. It wasn't because I was good or because my relationship with Him was so great. Neither of those were true. It was because His nature is to love. He *is* love.

God's nature is not limited to only loving me. His nature is to love you too. That's who He is. He loves each and every one of us. His love extends to the faithful and to the unbeliever just the same. It reaches from my living room to the other side of the world, from the classroom to the courtroom, and from congressional halls into prison walls. His love mends brokenness and heals wounds.

God's love *redeems*. His love *reconnects*. His love *restores*.

8

STRENGTH IN COMMUNITY

"Two are better than one, because they have a good reward for their toil. For if they fall, one will lift up his fellow. But woe to him who is alone when he falls and has not another to lift him up! Again, if two lie together, they keep warm, but how can one keep warm alone? And though a man might prevail against one who is alone, two will withstand him—a threefold cord is not quickly broken."

Ecclesiastes 4:9-12

It takes a village to raise a child. That village should not only be there to help raise the child and redirect when the child gets out of line,

Strength in Community

but the village also must be there to protect and guide the child to ensure that child can reach his or her full potential. A village needs all kinds of people to fill different roles. Our role doesn't have to be the greatest one. It need only be a working one. To help someone reach their dreams, your role can be as simple, yet meaningful, as a voice of encouragement. In whatever active role we take, the collective strength of family, friends, and community will yield positive results.

I would not have been able to move one step toward my goals without others' help. There were many people on my path from childhood to adulthood that played a role in my success. I lost some people somewhere along the path too. The people who start with us may not always be there when we finish. And that's okay. It seems to happen often on long journeys. I've learned to grow and thrive in those losses, too. The people we lose will reconnect with us if it's God's will.

Independent Woman

My dad raised me to be independent. Many African American parents raise their children this way. Other than him, I couldn't ask anybody else for anything, especially not for money. I took this mindset with me throughout most of my life.

At some point after marriage, I realized it was okay to ask for help. Yes, you read that correctly. It wasn't until after marriage that I finally realized there was nothing wrong with asking for help. I still struggle with it, but it has become easier. Before then, I was uncomfortable, and I felt a sense of indebtedness to someone who helped me. It always felt weird for people to do nice things for me. What was their motive? Would they hold this over my head? How am I to repay them? I should be able to do this alone! Those were my thoughts.

I'm happy my dad taught me how to be independent. We should all strive to teach this to our children. But there is a point where they must understand when it is okay to ask for help. We place them at a significant disadvantage when we teach them that they need to be *completely* independent to make it in life. We hold them back when we make them feel like they don't deserve the help they need to succeed. It should be the norm and they should expect to have a village they can depend on.

Years ago, while very ill with walking pneumonia, I was still trying to maintain my household, all while I could barely get out of bed. I remember vividly a Christian sister saying, *"April, let me help you. I want to help."*

Her actions demonstrated how God's mission is accomplished through everyday relationships; relationships that we sometimes take for granted. After that initial episode of going back and forth trying to explain why she didn't have to go out of her way to help, and how I could handle it myself, she just stopped asking. Instead, when she saw a need, she started *telling* me what she was going to do to help me.

"I'm bringing your family dinner this week."

She stopped giving me the opportunity to awkwardly explain that I was "good" or to tell her why she didn't *have* to do what she was asking to do. It became easier for me to just say "*Okay.*"

I've started using this effective approach.

Staying on the Right Track

Today I realize that I absolutely needed the help of people who took their time and utilized their resources to give me the opportunity to succeed. My dad was one of those people. He had high expectations. He set the bar high and dared me not to clear it. It wasn't easy, but I knew he meant business.

For example, he expected me to perform at a certain level in school. I did. There were no questions about it. He expected me to keep the house maintained. I did that, too. I might have griped about it, but what child *wants* to clean up? He expected my brothers and me to go to church, even if he didn't go and even if he didn't take us; which meant, many times, we walked or rode our bikes. Guess what? We were at church, and on time. His parenting style was strict, but it may have been the structure I needed to help keep me on the right track.

There were several instances in my life when I did get off track. I did things I should not have done, but my dad's expectations kept a spot in the back of my mind. I could have gone down a more extreme path that would've been consistent with the circumstances and environments I lived in as a child, but there was a line I would not cross. I knew my limits. Today, I'm thankful for that.

The promising part about my dad's expectations was that when I couldn't do it by myself his expectations were met with his actions. He expected me to attain a certain level of education so when I struggled with my newborn son away from home in college, he helped me regroup by moving our entire family into a house in the same city as my college. That meant going through the process of transferring his Section 8 housing voucher and moving himself and my younger brothers one hundred miles away from home. He made sure I had the support I needed to get over a major roadblock that could have easily derailed my progress.

In addition to my dad, there was always someone else helping to steer me in the right direction. Throughout the years of struggling after high school, I thought many times about the people who encouraged me during my childhood.

I thought about my late great-aunt who always had a smile and greeted me so warmly every time I walked through the church doors. I thought about the staff at our local Boys and Girls Club who showed us they cared and wanted us to succeed. The small scholarship I was awarded after being named Boys and Girls Club Youth of the Year was the first thing that piqued my interest in going to college. From the time I received the scholarship in 7th grade I was motivated about going to college. I felt obligated to use the scholarship. I didn't want it to go to waste.

The encouraging words I received in middle school from the Boys and Girls Club Board President, who told me I could be the first Black President (long before it became a reality!), played over in my mind. Memories of a local realtor taking me on a shopping spree for winning Youth of the Year made my heart smile. I thought about my childhood teachers and community members and so many others who challenged me and pushed me because they had hope and saw promise in me.

When I went to law school, I had people like my son's grandparents who selflessly took him in to live with them until I finished my first year, despite that I was no longer in a relationship with their son. They were more support than I could have asked for. They took my son to school, fed him, made sure he did his homework, put him in extracurricular activities and all the other things that parents do for their child, except this wasn't *their* child.

I felt a sense of guilt for leaving my son to pursue my dreams. For the time he was away, my mind consistently went back to my childhood when I was without my mother. I tried to rationalize it (thinking the sacrifice would ultimately make life better for him), but I still ended back at the fact that I had left him. Knowing he was in safe hands with them gave me some solace.

Encouraging Strength

College was hard, but I never considered quitting. Law school was a different story. I almost quit during my first year because it was too much. On top of the rigorous coursework and the guilt of not having my son with me, I was flat out broke. That made matters worse, and I slid into depression. At my lowest point, I had people like my stepdad and my now husband, who encouraged me to stick it out.

There were so many times when things could have gone a different way. Thank God for the strength that came with the help and encouragement from those so close to me.

We should always be able depend on close family and friends to help us reach our goals. Sometimes we may even have to depend on people we never would have imagined. When I was getting ready to go off to college, I didn't have childcare for my four-month-old. It would have been impossible for me to go to school with no one to take care of him.

A church member gave my dad the name of a woman who might have been able to babysit my child while I was in school. I did not know this lady at all. My dad did not know her either. All I knew was that she was a member of the church, and I rested on that. I was still nervous though.

For one, I didn't know how she would treat my son. I also discovered she lived in one of the worst housing projects in the city. I almost said forget it altogether. But when I went into her home to meet her, I felt a sense of calm. She was very nice and had a wonderful spirit. However, in all honesty, I was still afraid to take him and drop him off every day because of where she lived. I was young and defenseless, but I had to have faith that he was in good hands; indeed, he was.

A Reason and a Season

God places people in our lives for a reason and some for a season. There are two women I know were hand-picked for both a reason and a season of my life. During one of the toughest points in my law school career, they made ways for me that others could not. They were my advocates at every turn!

One was the director who hired me for my federal government job. She extended so much grace to me when she knew I was struggling in my last year of law school. I was pregnant, commuting almost two hours each way to the job, studying for the Bar, and trying to get the required number of work hours to be converted to a full-time position. Not just that, once we finally moved closer to my job, we lived in a hotel for weeks until we could close on our home. During those weeks, our lives were so unstable, and I could never complete an entire work-day. She worked with me though.

She would not allow me to be lost by the wayside. She didn't just give me a job. She made sure I kept it and excelled in it. I would not have been able to enjoy a successful federal career without her help. We worked in the same office together for probably only a year before she moved – just a season.

Judge P. Luevonda Ross was another woman I know God used at the right time. She was my law school professor-mom. Not only did she teach me the law and how to vigorously defend my position in the courtroom, she gave me that shoulder (and desk) to cry on when I felt the walls caving in. She didn't just listen. She offered solutions.

She knew I was going to quit law school because I didn't have enough money to survive, so she offered me her Research Assistant position. The extra money gave me a little breathing room. I identified with her and she empathized with me. I never realized the importance of diversity and representation in prominent positions until then. I needed someone like me to be a voice for me. Though she has transitioned from this side of life, her legacy and encouragement live on through me.

At each point in my life, I had people who set expectations, encouraged me and who held me accountable. We must do the same for our children and the children of our community.

Under the eyes of the law, our children are considered our "dependents" until they reach a certain age. They depend on us for their basic needs: clothing, shelter, food, and education. There can be legal consequences if we neglect to provide those basic needs to our children. But just as they depend on us for the basics, they also depend on us for guidance, direction, and encouragement. My dad certainly wasn't a perfect parent; however, he came to understand that he not only had to provide for me physically, but he had to put me in the best position for life.

Strength in Community

We won't be perfect parents, aunts, uncles, cousins, or friends, but we can be a source of strength for our children and the children in our lives. We can inspire them to be the best they can be. They need to know we expect greatness from them!

Our expectations should be met with our actions as well. We must set the bar high and encourage them along the way; encourage them through the good and bad choices they make. When they make good choices, we should offer rewards and incentives, like the Boys and Girls Club scholarship awarded to me in middle school. However, when they make bad choices we must hold them accountable.

We want our future generation to be better. I've heard it said time and time again, *"I don't want you to be like me; be better than me."* However, we can't just say those words. We have to show our children what that means specifically.

God uses ordinary people to do His work as He has done since the beginning of time. He

Only the Strong Thrive

places ordinary people in our lives to help us in extraordinary ways. Those people may not only be in our close family or community. At times it could be people we may not even know. There are people in each of our lives who are ready and willing to help us reach our goals and aspirations.

9

THE STRENGTH TO MOVE FORWARD

"Not that I have already obtained this or am already perfect, but I press on to make it my own, because Christ Jesus has made me his own. Brothers, I do not consider that I have made it my own. But one thing I do: forgetting what lies behind and straining forward to what lies ahead, I press on toward the goal for the prize of the upward call of God in Christ Jesus."

Philippians 3:12-14

As long as we are here on this earth, there's always a next chapter; always more for us to do. Moving forward means different things for each of us based on our wants and needs. For some, moving forward may mean letting go of a relationship, while it may mean holding on to one for others.

For all of us, striving for a more intimate relationship with God should always be a part of our moving forward. Climbing to higher heights with Him should be our goal. He desires to have that relationship with us, and He will reveal where He is leading us when we seek His face. He wants to lead us to a place where we can live confidently and bring glory to Him. I wish I had realized earlier in life that living confidently in Jesus Christ doesn't mean living perfectly.

Our quest for perfection can cause us unnecessary pressure. I'm guilty of it. I've caused myself both healthy and unhealthy pressure. There's nothing wrong with healthy pressure. Healthy pressure kept me moving toward my goals, despite the circumstances. It was my motivation.

Unhealthy pressure only kept me moving in

circles. That kind of pressure pushes us into exhaustion, for the sake of perfection. When we feel we haven't achieved perfection (which we rarely do), we doubt ourselves. In our doubt, it's good to be reminded that we don't need to be perfect, even if that reminder comes from the most unlikely person.

Everything Doesn't Have to Be Perfect

I've wanted to have children since I was a very little girl. My cousin and I played pretend all the time. We planned our children's genders, we named them, and imagined what close friends our children would be. I really wanted to have girls, so I could comb their hair and do fun "girly" things. I was eager to shop for hair bows and hair products. I was hopeful I'd get to sit my daughters on my lap and perfectly style their hair for the day. I envisioned it being fun and easy. I believed I would be the kind of mother who combed and brushed my daughters' hair every day.

Then, I actually had a daughter. And not just

one, I had two. Two heads to try to comb and style. I now had to find double the time to devote just to combing hair. Finding the time became harder and harder as the years rolled by. At some point, I realized I wasn't really good at styling their hair either.

To make matters worse, my youngest daughter does not enjoy having her hair combed one bit. She cries louder than a hungry newborn anytime I even attempt to comb her hair. Her tears don't start when I touch her hair but before, just around the time I mention the word "comb." It's exhausting.

Many times, I've sat with them combing, brushing, and moisturizing over and over until I have to stop - and realize it will never be as "perfect" as I want it to be. Thinking back, it's funny that I thought combing hair was going to be the best time of my parenting experience.

Thankfully, these experiences with my children have been one of the best things to tamp down my craving for perfection. My oldest daughter, at 4 years old, first reminded me that perfection is not required. Leave it to her to call me out on it.

"Mom, everything doesn't have to be perfect."

Until that time, I didn't really understand or even see how unhealthy my craving for perfection was. I'd experienced too many failures. I wanted everything to be right, but it wasn't necessary. There's a way to hold ourselves to a high standard, but it is also okay to extend ourselves a little grace.

One of my dear Christian sisters summed it up perfectly for me one day several years ago when she said, *"April, be excellent, not perfect."* Her words were everything. I've learned so much from her wisdom, but on this day her words struck me in a way that really spoke to me. Somehow, she knew what I needed to hear.

When I reflected on her statement, I realized I had a false sense of perfection. I wanted everything around me to be perfect. I sought perfection in things that did not matter. Does God care whether my daughter's hair is styled perfectly? Does He care whether she has the perfect bow to match her outfit? Not only did I want perfection in things that did not matter, but I wanted perfection in things I couldn't control. I had to move away from that thinking.

Moving away from a desire for perfection doesn't mean we should lower our standards. We can be excellent, and we can be exceptional. We should put our very best into everything we do–in our service to God, in our marriages, in raising our children, in school, in our work, in serving the community, and so on. We thrive when we are at our best.

Moving Forward in Excellence

To move forward in excellence we must be conscious of our decisions. For the most part, many of the decisions we make on a day to day basis don't matter much. Although we sometimes put a lot of time and effort into day to day activities, like finding the perfect outfit to wear, it will likely not have any matter of importance on our tomorrow. However, there are other more important decisions that will lead us on the right path to accomplishing our goals. Even some decisions that we may consider "minor" can lead us in the right direction; while others can put us on a path that will make it harder to get to our desired place in life.

The minor decisions set us *apart* from others, and the major ones set us *up* for success. Some of those major decisions may involve risks. If we took no risks at all, we wouldn't be able to strengthen our "faith muscles." We wouldn't allow God to work in the way He works. We wouldn't allow His strength to work in us.

I've taken a few big risks that have allowed me to be where I am today. The first risk was starting college classes one day after my first child was born. The next risk was packing him up four months later and moving miles away from my family to attend college.

I left the comfort of a place I'd lived for most

of my life to move to an unfamiliar city and into an uncomfortable campus apartment alone, with an infant. The apartments, which were reserved for students with families, were extremely outdated and set to be demolished that same year. No matter how nice I tried to fix up the apartment, the atmosphere was never welcoming. The concrete floors were so cold. I never felt at home there.

I was a new mom, with an infant, in a new city, and I was lonely. Since there wasn't much I was going to be able to do on campus with a baby, we were in bed every night before 8 p.m. It was tough. I didn't even make it through the full semester before I had to reconsider what I'd gotten myself and my baby into.

Taking a Step Back

I realized I wasn't stable enough as a 19-year-old small city girl to be living in a big city with an infant. After discussing it with my dad and our associate minister, I moved back home. Although it was one of the best decisions I could've made, knowing that after I'd packed up my four-month-old, loaded a U-Haul with furniture, clothes, toys, and everything else, that just a few months later I was packing back up to go home was surreal.

Thankfully, my dad welcomed me home with open arms. I never once heard "I told you so." He never discussed the wasted time, money or energy in getting me down there and back.

Although it seemed like a move backward, it gave me a glimpse of what I could look forward to. I had to move back to be able to move forward. My time away in college for those few months wasn't all for naught, though. I moved back home, but I wouldn't give up that easily. The whole semester didn't have to go to waste, so I commuted back and forth to complete it.

For the time I was back home after that semester, I attended classes at the community college where I started. I felt like I was going in circles. My mind was flooded with the negative statements I heard right after revealing my pregnancy. I knew people expected me to fail. It was most humbling to sit on the church pews on

Sunday morning because I knew much of the talk came from within those walls.

However, I was determined to make it back to the university. A year later, I had the courage and stability to try it again. This time, I had the strength to move forward with my dad and my brothers by my side. We made it a family affair.

Imperfect Path

An imperfect path doesn't have to stop our journeys. There is much to be learned and gained from our imperfect lives. My college journey taught me there can be more than one path to a desired goal. The path we initially choose may not be the path we ultimately take, but resilience and perseverance are vital. We must resolve to keep going, regardless of how rocky the road becomes.

The imperfect childhood that my brothers and I endured together only made us stronger.

The Strength to Move Forward

We needed one another's support, especially during the hardest moments in our childhood. At times we felt like we only had each other. Today we share a treasured bond and we truly value the roles that we play in one another's lives.

Through my parent's imperfect and failed relationship, I've learned the importance of global commitment in marriage and in parenting. The commitment should not only be shared between family in the same household, but extended family and friends should share a similar commitment to that family. There is strength in numbers. Sometimes the extra encouragement and support that might come from outside our homes is the reassurance we need to keep our families together.

Moving forward doesn't mean moving perfectly in a straight line. Sometimes it means taking a step back to reassess where we are and where we need to be. It requires a serious and honest evaluation of the situation we're in.

It may be advantageous to seek advice from

experienced, wise, and trusted individuals. We shouldn't be down on ourselves if we have to take a step back. We may not always hit the target on the first try. Stepping back to reassess where we are may be necessary to put us in a better position to aim the next time.

10

THE STRENGTH TO TRIUMPH

"Now thanks be to God who always leads us in triumph in Christ, and through us spreads the fragrance of the knowledge of him everywhere."

2 Corinthians 2:14

I've wanted to become an attorney since I can remember. Legal investigations, forensics, and the presentation of evidence in court intrigued me so much as a young girl that I would constantly watch live trials and other court shows on television. My dad would always say I needed to be an attorney because I was very opinionated and strong-minded. I don't think either of us realized it then, but I was destined to be exactly where I am in my career right now.

Today, I am one of nearly fifteen thousand attorneys licensed to practice law in Alabama. Seven percent, or about one thousand and fifty attorneys, are African American. An even smaller percentage are African American women.

Becoming an attorney is a significant accomplishment for *anyone* who's able to achieve that goal. The statistics suggest it is even *more* significant for someone who looks like me. It is an extremely difficult process. Once students enter law school, they have to successfully cross several bridges on their journey to become an attorney.

The first bridge is the dreaded first year. If you know someone who's been down that road, they would probably tell you if you can survive the first year of law school, you have all but guaranteed yourself a seat at graduation. That is not to say the second and third years are easy, but there is nothing like the demand and rigor of the first year. It is a beast.

The first year not only changed me intellectually, but it changed me physically, emotionally, and mentally. I lost twenty pounds, nearly lost a boyfriend, and almost lost my mind all in that same year.

After successfully completing each of the three years, graduation is the next stop. Graduation was one of the most triumphant, yet tense, experiences along my journey to becoming an attorney. As joyous and celebratory as it was, the anxiety of taking the biggest exam of my life was hanging over me. I couldn't rest in the fact that I had just graduated and received my law degree. My classmates probably felt the same way, but I had another reason to be nervous.

Only the Strong Thrive

I was going to be eight months pregnant when the State Bar Exam was to be administered. The exam consisted of two full days and one-half day of writing essays and responding to numerous multiple-choice questions. I was uneasy about sitting in an exam chair for hours at a time in my late stage of pregnancy.

Then there were questions from some of my well-meaning friends.

"What if your water breaks during the exam?"

I'd most often respond, *"You better keep writing because I'm surely going to!"*

I had convinced myself that if my water broke during the exam, someone would have to force me out on a stretcher while I was still writing. I could not see myself going out quietly after all I had to endure to get there. I had studied 8-10 hours nearly every day for over two months. I did not want to take that test again.

It would have made for a great story had I been forced to finish my exam while in route to a hospital but thank God that is not my story to tell. I made it through the exhausting three days. However, it wasn't over.

The exam results were scheduled to be released a couple of months later, so I'd have to wait to know the results. We were moving to a city closer to my job a couple of days after the exam, so I couldn't dwell on it much. I was preoccupied with packing, moving, buying a house, enrolling my son into a new school, and... having a baby! Worry about the bar exam results would have to take a back seat.

Victory in Jesus

Weeks after the exam, as I lay next to my one-week-old daughter, my phone buzzed. It was a text from my friend.

"Check the bar website."

My heart stopped. One part of me knew he

wouldn't text a one-week-postpartum mother at 8 a.m. to tell me I didn't pass the exam, but the other side of me thought he might have wanted to rub it in my face that he had passed, and I hadn't.

I quickly rolled over and pulled up my laptop which seemed to take forever to load. As I hurriedly typed my name into the member directory search on the State Bar website, my heart started pumping overtime. It was about to explode! Finally, what I had been waiting for months to know: I was listed on the state bar attorney roll! With my sleeping newborn lying in bed beside me, I let out a big yelp and cry! I could not contain myself.

"Wow, I did it!"

It was a huge achievement!

Graduating law school, passing the bar exam, and becoming an attorney were big accomplishments that I worked hard to achieve. They are achievements I will cherish forever, but I don't count them as my most significant victories. I am victorious and blessed because I have the support and love of family and friends. I have a devoted husband and my children have a loving father. I enjoy a fruitful career where I can help change people's lives. I am walking in my purpose.

My victory is in Jesus Christ. The strength I was able to tap into throughout my journey was His strength. Through my earthly victories, I'm able to spread the knowledge of Christ. I can testify about God's goodness and His marvelous works. The world will know I was able to victoriously overcome through Him. My gift in return is to spread the knowledge of Him, His love, and His strength to all I know.

When we began in Chapter 1, I posed the question "To thrive or to survive?" Though it's a question that we each have to answer for ourselves, I truly believe we all would answer the same way. No one really *wants* to just survive. We all want to *thrive*. We want to win at life. Each of us wants to wake up every day with purpose, live our lives to the fullest, and leave legacies our children can be proud of. Through our victories, our children will know they can also thrive.

Decide to Thrive

We can thrive despite adversity. Our starting point doesn't determine where we'll finish. Fear will tell us a different story, but we can conquer those fears. Our faith will guide us when we don't know where to turn. It isn't necessary to move perfectly through life. Honestly, perfection isn't possible. We will hit speedbumps. Regardless of what happens though, we must continue forward.

Before we can move forward, we must learn to accept our circumstances and own who we are and where we are. An easier way to say it is we must learn to *walk in our truth.* Once we're walking in our truth, we can make sound decisions and take the required actions to move us in a positive direction.

We have all we need to achieve. Inner motivation and perseverance are qualities we all possess. I didn't always think I had the necessary tools or qualities to succeed, but I learned to dig deep into those assets throughout my journey.

My journey wasn't only mine. It is a testimony for anyone who has experienced struggles. My journey is proof that you can overcome *any* obstacle, whether the obstacle was placed before you or whether you stumbled over your own two feet. No matter the circumstance, victory is yours! God's love, grace, and mercy covers you like it has covered me.

I did not understand why my path was so difficult. I don't know why it was the path chosen for me, but I'm at peace with it now. I'm at peace with the circumstances in my childhood that forced me to grow up faster than I wanted to. I could not control those years, but I could control how I allowed them to impact my future.

In the midst of hard times, I made the decision not to accept whatever life threw at me. I chose to make life what I wanted. The best way to make our lives what we truly want is to allow

Only the Strong Thrive

God to make our lives what He wants. He wants the best for us. Others may not. Sometimes, we may not even understand what is best for our own lives. We can't always see the bigger picture.

Our decision to take control of our futures may be met with resistance sometimes. Circumstances, environments, and people try to deter us from the abundant life Christ promised. However, we shouldn't accept anything less than His promise.

We've been given the power and authority to live abundant lives. We don't need anyone's approval, and we don't have to wait on it. Make your own way. Live the life you've been promised.

Thrive!

Acknowledgments
My Community

Not one word in this book would have been possible without God's love, mercy, and grace. Thank you, Father for your promise of abundant life on earth and in Heaven.

My Husband, Quincy:

I don't have the words to express my love and gratitude to you. We have grown so much together, and the journey is one I will take again, several times over. I thank God we crossed paths on that cold January night. Thank you for the encouragement to chase each and every little "crazy" dream that pops up in my mind. Thank you for every second you put into making this book what it is. I love you with all that I am.

My Children, Jaylen, Ava, Aryn & Warren:

You have given my life meaning. You have each changed me in a different way, for the better. My focus, determination and drive were because of you. You are why I am who I am. You have brought me the greatest joy in life and I pray that you spread that same joy to all who cross your path. Glorify God in all that you do. I love you.

My Mom, Sheraton:

I don't know what I would do if you were not in my life. I am so thankful our relationship has grown significantly over the years. I know I can always call on you and you will come running. Only God could have predicted we would be here today. Love never fails. It never gives up. Thank you for not giving up.

My Daddy, Valentino:

I am so blessed to have a father who went so hard for us.

Only the Strong Thrive

I got my "hustle" spirit from you, although I like to call it perseverance. I am totally who I am today and where I am because of the time you took to raise me right, even when I made mistakes and it became tiring, you didn't give up on me. Thank you for it all.

My Step-Dad, Greg:

From the first day I've known you, you have been nothing but supportive. Thank you for encouraging me to keep going when I felt like giving up.

My Brothers: Antwone, Tino, & Myles

You guys are the only ones who really and truly understand those days on Scotland Drive, in the sub, the duplex, and in BD because you lived through it too. Thank God I had each of you to grow up with. I'm a blessed woman to have brothers who are there for me in every way. I love you guys.

My Grandmother, Margaret:

I can always count on you to be there with bells and whistles no matter what. Your home has always been a safe haven. Thank you for that. I appreciate your consistent love and support.

My Cousin, K'yani:

All I need to say is "You know." You know and understand it all. From our duplex sleepy prayers and dreams, to our BD years, to our college roommate days, you have been there. We didn't get to live next door to each other, but I guess living together in college will have to suffice. Thank you for being the sister I always wanted and needed.

My Granddaddy, Roosevelt:

If there wasn't anyone in my childhood that I could count on, I could count on you. You were there at the drop

Acknowledgments

of a dime. I still remember your phone number from thirty years ago. You are forever in my heart. You earned your crown. I pray to see you again in Heaven.

John & Pam:

You are two of the most genuine and loving people I know. From the day I met both of you, before even knowing what would follow, you treated me kindly and with the utmost respect. Our relationship grew even stronger after Jaylen came along. I adore both of you. I will never be able to repay you for all that you have done.

My Extended Family (Houston & Jones Families):

Aunts, uncles, and cousins, thank you all for the laughs, the joys and each memorable moment. I appreciate your support in every way. I'd run out of space if I named each of you individually but know that I love you and hold each of you dear to my heart. Some of you first cousins know a lot of this story because you were basically like brothers and sister. (Rodd, Ashley, Tr'maine, and Mookie)

My In-Laws:

One asset of marriage is the blessing of family gained. Each of you have enriched my life, and I am more than blessed because of it. Thank you, to my mother and father-in-law, Walter and Geraldine, for the love you have shown and for raising a son to know how to love and care for others. Coretta, Floyd, Erica, Gary, Audrey, and Adrian: We each share our own special and unique relationships. Thank you for the love of family.

Special Christian Sisters:

Felicia, I can never repay you for the encouragement and the vision you spoke over me to start writing my book. I knew I had a book inside, I just needed someone to push it out of me. I am encouraged by how you allow the Holy

Spirit to work in and through you. I know God hears every prayer you have prayed for me and my family. Adena, every word you have spoken to me from the beginning of our friendship has been positive, inspirational, loving, and to make me a better Christian. "Be excellent, not perfect" were words spoken at a time when I needed to hear it most. You've taught me so much about this Christian walk, being a Christian wife and mother. Tri'Sheena, thank you for the Bible Study that we both needed but may not have realized at the time. This book is completed because of it. Our sisterhood means so much.

The Boys & Girls Club:

So many of you showed me and the other club members that you cared and wanted us to be successful. Chris R., I don't know what you saw in me so many years ago but thank God your inspiration stayed with me through my teenage and adult years. I am so grateful we had the opportunity to reconnect years ago. Mr. Williams, Mrs. Rainey-Thompson, and the other staff who spent your days ensuring we had experiences to remember. Because of you, the Boys and Girls Club had a positive impact on my life. Karen B, thank you for rewarding me with the shopping spree as a young girl years ago. Your act of kindness has stayed with me for so many years.

Natasha W.:

I would not be where I am in my career without your help. Thank you for giving me a chance and for extending grace when I needed it most.

Friends & Sorors:

I have been tremendously blessed to have people who are not blood kin but who love me just the same. Britney, we've been going strong for nearly 20 years! When I say, "best

Acknowledgments

friend," you are who I am speaking of. Your friendship has been solid. Thank you for always being there. To the ladies of Alpha Kappa Alpha, Sorority, Inc., and Mesmerizing 26: What would I do without you? I am thankful for the many years of sisterhood. Special smooches to my three amigas, Shauna, Monica, and Mirica.

Hoover Church of Christ Family:

One of the hardest things for my family after we moved was finding a church home. We found a true gem when we stumbled upon Hoover one Sunday. Our quality of life has tremendously increased as a result. A special thanks to Nikesha, Doris, Iesha, Teresa H. and Teresa R. for the extra-special bond we've shared over the years.

Advance Readers:

You could have spent your time doing many other things. While juggling work, travel, pregnancy, a dissertation, and many other projects, you took the time to read this book and provide excellent feedback. I am forever grateful to you: Quincey, Debra, Jamie, Chuck, Susan, and Sheila.

April (Houston) Collins was raised in Athens, Alabama where she was active in many school activities, clubs and organizations. She attended the Athens Boys and Girls Club and was named Boys & Girls Club Youth of the Year. Shortly after graduating from high school, she and her 4-month old son moved to Birmingham, Alabama, so she could attend the University of Alabama at Birmingham (UAB).

After graduating from UAB, she enrolled into law school at Faulkner University. As a law student, she was awarded the Justice Janie L. Shores Scholarship, named in honor of the first female Alabama Supreme Court Justice. April was also elected to serve on the Editorial Board of the

About the Author

Faulkner Law Review. Of the seven Board members elected, April was the only African-American and the only female Board member. Her case note *You Be the Judge: Avoiding Attorney Discipline by Taking the Bench* was also published in the law review.

While in law school, April had the unique opportunity to intern for two judges, while also working as a research assistant to one of her professors. After graduating from law school and passing the Alabama State Bar exam, April was offered a career position as a Federal Investigator with the U.S. Department of Housing and Urban Development.

Shortly thereafter, Athens Mayor proclaimed a day in April's honor, while presenting her with a key to the city. Just a few months later, she was inducted into the North Alabama Boys & Girls Club Hall of Fame. After five years, April left the federal government and took the plunge to start her own law firm, Collins Law, LLC, focusing primarily on civil rights and personal injury law.

April is married and has four children. She and her family are members of the Hoover Church of Christ in Hoover, Alabama.

SHARE _YOUR_ STORY ALONGSIDE FRIENDS WITH THE APPLICATION JOURNAL

With this application journal you can process each chapter of this book in your own way, tackling each issue in the way that suits your situation.

Complete with Bible verses, prompts, questions, and plenty of space to express your feelings in free writing, this journal forms a vital part of your journey. The strength to overcome life's challenges is already within you. With this accompaniment to *Only the Strong Thrive* you can use your strength to build the future you want.

ONLYTHESTRONGTHRIVE.COM

Made in the USA
Lexington, KY
24 October 2018